SUMMER & WINTER
SIMPLY

SUMMER & WINTER
SIMPLY

UNDERSTANDING THE WEAVE STRUCTURE

34 PROJECTS TO PRACTICE YOUR SKILLS

SUSAN KESLER-SIMPSON

STACKPOLE
BOOKS

Essex, Connecticut
Blue Ridge Summit, Pennsylvania

STACKPOLE BOOKS

An imprint of The Globe Pequot Publishing Group, Inc.
64 South Main Street
Essex, CT 06426
www.globepequot.com

Distributed by NATIONAL BOOK NETWORK
800-462-6420

Copyright © 2025 by Susan Kesler-Simpson

Photography by Eckhaus Images, except pages 67, 69, and 127 by Susan Kesler-Simpson

All rights reserved. No part of this book may be reproduced in any form or by any electronic or mechanical means, including information storage and retrieval systems, without written permission from the publisher, except by a reviewer who may quote passages in a review.

The contents of this book are for personal use only. Patterns herein may be reproduced in limited quantities for such use. Any large-scale commercial reproduction is prohibited without the written consent of the publisher.

We have made every effort to ensure the accuracy and completeness of these instructions. We cannot, however, be responsible for human error, typographical mistakes, or variations in individual work.

British Library Cataloguing in Publication Information available

Library of Congress Cataloging-in-Publication Data

Names: Kesler-Simpson, Susan, author.
Title: Summer and winter simply / Susan Kesler-Simpson.
Description: First edition. | Essex, Connecticut ; Blue Ridge Summit, Pennsylvania : Stackpole Books, [2025] | Includes bibliographical references. | Summary: "'Summer and Winter' refers to the weave's characteristic look of one light side and one dark side. In this new book, Susan Kesler-Simpson breaks down the weave structure to make it easy to understand and includes 34 projects including shawls, blankets, table linens, and dish towels"— Provided by publisher.
Identifiers: LCCN 2024027847 (print) | LCCN 2024027848 (ebook) | ISBN 9780811772846 (paperback) | ISBN 9780811772853 (epub)
Subjects: LCSH: Hand weaving. | Hand weaving—Patterns.
Classification: LCC TT848 .K475 2025 (print) | LCC TT848 (ebook) | DDC 746.1/4—dc23/eng/20240916
LC record available at https://lccn.loc.gov/2024027847
LC ebook record available at https://lccn.loc.gov/2024027848

♾️™ The paper used in this publication meets the minimum requirements of American National Standard for Information Sciences—Permanence of Paper for Printed Library Materials, ANSI/NISO Z39.48-1992.

First Edition

CONTENTS

Introduction 1

CHAPTER 1: Summer and Winter 3

CHAPTER 2: Multi-Pedal Treadling for a Jack Loom 13

CHAPTER 3: Profile Drafts 16

CHAPTER 4: Fiber and Color 22

Resources 135

PROJECTS

4-SHAFT PROJECTS 25

Autumn Splendor
Placemat and Napkins **27**

Footpath
Table Runner **29**

Purple Haze Scarf
33

Sea Glass
Table Runner **35**

Sherbet Scarf
39

Towels Three Ways
41

Tiny Blocks Scarf
45

Just for Fun
Table Runner **47**

8-SHAFT PROJECTS 57

Caribbean Nights Shawl **51**

Scarves for Karen **53**

Blue Cubed Table Runner **59**

Bones Towels **61**

Boo! Scarf **65**

Christmas Lights Towels **69**

Circle of Roses Scarf **73**

Coffee and Cream Scarf **75**

Color Play Placemat **79**

Easter Eggs One and Two Table Runners **81**

Birthday Celebration Table Runner **85**

Eire Spring Table Runner **89**

Lace Runner **91**

Peaks and Valleys Scarf **95**

Peonies Scarf **99**

Pinwheels Scarf
101

Scarf Set
105

Seasons
Table Runner **107**

Shades of Green Scarf
111

Sunspots
Table Runner **113**

Woodland Runner
117

Smitten with Kittens
Table Runner **121**

Hanukkah Runner
123

Bunches of Bunnies
Blanket **127**

Just a Wrap
129

Going in Style Trim
133

CONTENTS | vii

INTRODUCTION

Life is a journey, sometimes taking you down paths you never planned to go. That has been our life this last year. Losing a portion of our home to a fire and being displaced created a tremendous amount of uncertainty and angst. Weaving was my link to sanity. Although I was unable to save my fiber, I did save my looms. And my weaving books, thank goodness! Thanks to a weaving friend, we were able to move into a fully furnished home with lots of room for us, Peanut our cat, and the looms. During this time, I taught my husband to weave. I'm not sure he is totally hooked on it, but he has a new appreciation for the craft. And he is a very good weaver!

As we waited for our home to be put back together, we had a lot of time on our hands. This was the perfect opportunity to do some in-depth studies on a few weave structures that were on my list. Summer and winter was at the top of that list. I immersed myself in the books on summer and winter and spent an afternoon with Tom Knisely to confirm my thoughts. It was at that point I decided that another "Simply" book was in the making, which would once again provide the weaver with just the basics in a manner that was easy to understand. As always, I also created a number of projects for the weaver to try out their new skills. I have found that once a weaver has successfully finished a project in a specific weave structure, their understanding of that weave structure strengthens and increases.

I am so thankful for my husband, Dave, who encouraged me in every way. He even wove some of the projects for this book. And a huge thanks to Tom Knisely, who has been a good friend and guiding force in my weaving journey. Enjoy!

CHAPTER 1

Summer and Winter

It is an unusual name for a weave pattern, right? So where did this name come from? Summer and winter was often used in antique coverlets. One of the most recognizable attributes of summer and winter is that one side of the piece is predominately light, while the opposite side is predominately dark. Tradition says that this arrangement was because it was more difficult to do laundry in the winter (remember, there weren't modern washing machines yet), so folks displayed the dark side during the cold months, as it didn't show the dirt as much. Then, in the summer, when it was easier to do laundry, the lighter side was on top. The light color would also brighten the room. I always liked this description. Being raised on a dairy farm, I remember that doing laundry was an issue. The old wringer washer was in the basement, and clothes were hung inside to dry in the winter. Not convenient! It is easy to see how this naming tradition could well have some basis in history.

Summer and winter also has the wonderful capability of creating images in the weave. I'm sure you have seen table runners, coverlets, and other projects with trees, flowers, and other image motifs. And, oh, how we love those! The ability to create images is limited only by the number of shafts on the loom.

Another recognizable feature of summer and winter is that none of the floats are more than three threads. This quality can be an advantage if you are making a baby blanket and need to be aware of tiny toes and fingers catching threads.

In this chapter, we will cover what makes up summer and winter threading, treadling, and tie-up. There will be some repetition, so bear with me.

Summer and winter is a 2-tie-down unit weave. That certainly was a mouthful, wasn't it? What does that mean? It means that in summer and winter, threading shafts 1 and 2 are reserved as tie-down threads. So when you are setting up your loom, 25% of your threads will be on shaft 1 and 25% of your threads will be on shaft 2. The other 50% of the threads create the pattern and will be spread over the remaining shafts. I highly recommend that you count your heddles on each shaft before you start threading. It is not fun to move heddles once you have started the threading process!

Now on to weaving summer and winter. Just as when weaving overshot, in summer and winter you will follow each weft pattern thread with a tabby thread. The first tabby is created with shafts 1 and 2. The second tabby is created using the remaining shafts beginning with shaft 3. You will be creating a plain weave base for any woven piece that you make. If you look closely at some of the old summer and winter coverlets, you will see places where the pattern threads are worn away, leaving a plain weave cloth. The use of the tabby gives these pieces stability and durability.

So what is a unit weave? A unit weave is a weave pattern in which the *pattern* shafts within a block are not shared with any other pattern shafts in a different block. Simply said: shaft 3 is reserved for one pattern block, shaft 4 is reserved for one pattern block, and so on, depending on the number of shafts you have or are using. You will not use pattern shafts 3 and 4 within the same block in summer and winter. Look at the graphs that follow, and you can see that each pattern shaft is used for just one block. Note also that each

SUMMER AND WINTER | 3

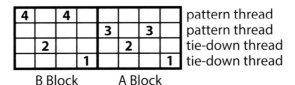

Figure 1.1 A 4-shaft loom allows you 2 pattern blocks.

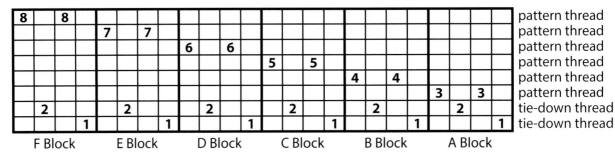

Figure 1.2 An 8-shaft loom allows you 6 pattern blocks.

block uses shafts 1 and 2 for tie-downs—hence the reason why summer and winter is called a 2-tie-down unit weave. The individual blocks are labeled A through F. Having more than 4 shafts is a definite advantage for summer and winter, as it gives you more blocks to design with. Using a 4-shaft loom allows you only 2 pattern blocks (Figure 1.1); an 8-shaft loom allows you 6 pattern blocks (Figure 1.2).

Summer and Winter Threading

Summer and winter is threaded in a very specific manner. Figure 1.3 shows the blocks for 8-shaft summer and winter. If you have a 4-shaft loom, you will be using only Blocks A and B. With an 8-shaft loom, you will use Blocks A through F.

Notice that each block has a thread on shaft 1 and a thread on shaft 2. These are the *tie-down* threads, as mentioned before. These threads do not add to the pattern but are background threads. They secure the pattern threads so that the floats are no longer than 3 threads.

Now notice that in Block A, there are 2 threads on shaft 3. Block B has 2 threads on shaft 4. This order continues through to Block F. These are your *pattern* threads. They will float over the surface, creating the design just as when you weave overshot. With a 4-shaft loom, you have only 2 blocks to use to create a pattern. But with 8 shafts, you have 6 blocks with which you can create patterns. Each additional shaft on your loom adds one more shaft to use for pattern creating. So for a 16-shaft loom, you would have 14 pattern threads. How fun would that be!

When you are creating a design, you should never reverse the arrangements of the threads within a block.

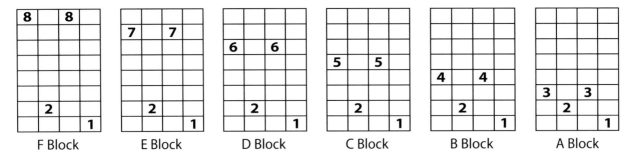

Figure 1.3 Summer and winter blocks for an 8-shaft loom; for a 4-shaft loom, you will use only Blocks A and B.

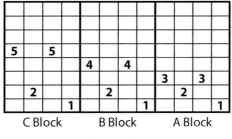

Figure 1.4

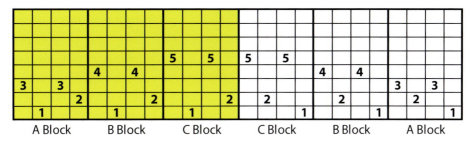

Figure 1.5

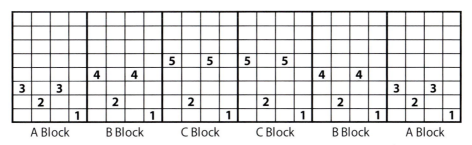

Figure 1.6

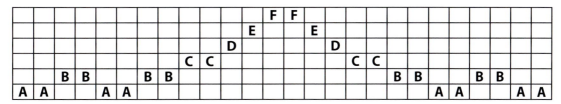

Figure 1.7 An example of a profile draft. Substitute the 4-thread blocks for each letter, as shown in Figure 1.3, for the complete threading.

Look at Figure 1.4. It consists of 3 blocks: A, B, and C. Let's assume that the C block is the turning point for this sequence.

If you are using a computer program and ask it to make your threading symmetrical, it will rearrange the blocks as in Figure 1.5.

But this is not correct! Notice that the positions of *all* of the threads have been rearranged in the second half highlighted in yellow. It is essential that each thread keep the same position within the block. The corrected graph is shown in Figure 1.6.

When you are writing out a draft by hand, it is unlikely that you will make this mistake. However, as handy as computer programs are, this is an area where they could create a problem. Use the copy and paste feature to prevent this mistake.

When you see a threading graph for summer and winter, you will rarely see that graph written out in full. The threading graph will most likely be written in what is referred to as a profile draft. Figure 1.7 shows an example of a profile draft. Be sure to read the chapter on profile drafts to understand how to use them if you are not familiar with them. Profile drafts are a wonderful shorthand tool for weavers. To see the complete threading draft, you would substitute the 4-thread block that is appropriate for each letter.

SUMMER AND WINTER | 5

Summer and Winter Treadling

Summer and winter also has specific treadling sequences. These treadling sequences are repeated one or more times, depending on your motif. Two of the treadling sequences—X's and O's—are made up of four components. There is a subtle difference between these two sequences, but it makes a big difference in appearance. There are also two additional treadling sequences that we will cover. And always remember that you will also insert a tabby thread after each pattern thread. Let's look at these different treadling sequences.

The first treadling sequence we will look at is the X sequence. Figure 1.8 shows this sequence along with the tie-up. Notice that the 4-thread treadling sequence is aligned with the corresponding pattern thread in the tie-up.

In this example, shafts 2 and 3 are raised, followed by shafts 1 and 3. Then shafts 1 and 3 are repeated, followed by shafts 2 and 3. This same treadling sequence is used with shafts 2 and 4 and shafts 1 and 4. Figure 1.9 shows a draft using the X treadling. This treadling sequence will remain the same regardless of the number of pattern shafts. Treadling in the X sequence creates a blockier image.

The next treadling sequence is the O sequence (Figure 1.10). The treadling begins with raising shafts 1 and 3, followed by shafts 2 and 3. Then shafts 2 and 3 are repeated, followed by shafts 1 and 3. The same treadling sequence is used with shafts 1 and 4 and shafts 2 and 4. This treadling sequence will remain the same regardless of the number of pattern shafts.

Figure 1.8 The X treadling sequence.

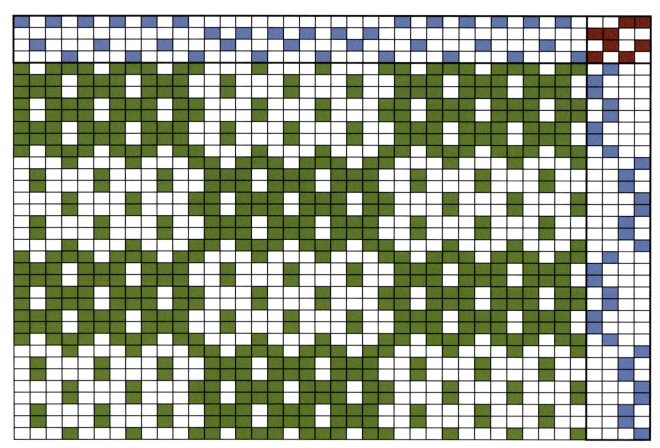

Figure 1.9 These pattern squares have sharp corners.

Figure 1.11 is the same draft as Figure 1.9 with O's treadling.

If you compare the corners of the blocks in Figures 1.9 and 1.11, you can see that the O's treadling sequence creates a rounded corner, whereas the corners in the X treadling sequence are sharper. So, which to use: the X's or the O's? It is a choice, and there is no wrong decision. It depends on the design you are working with and how you want your motif to look.

There are two more treadling sequences in summer and winter. The next treadling is the alternate treadling sequence, shown in Figure 1.12. Instead of repeating a treadling sequence of four, you will alternate raising shafts 1 and 3, followed by shafts 2 and 3. The same treadling sequence is used with shafts 1 and 4 and shafts 2 and 4. If you have more than 4 shafts, this treadling sequence remains the same.

Figure 1.13 shows how this treadling affects a design. You no longer see those doubles along the edge of the blocks. You can repeat as desired with this sequence and are not locked into completing a sequence of four. I like to use this treadling sequence when designing motifs.

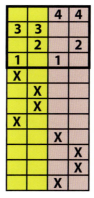

Figure 1.10 The O treadling sequence.

Figure 1.12 Alternate treadling sequence.

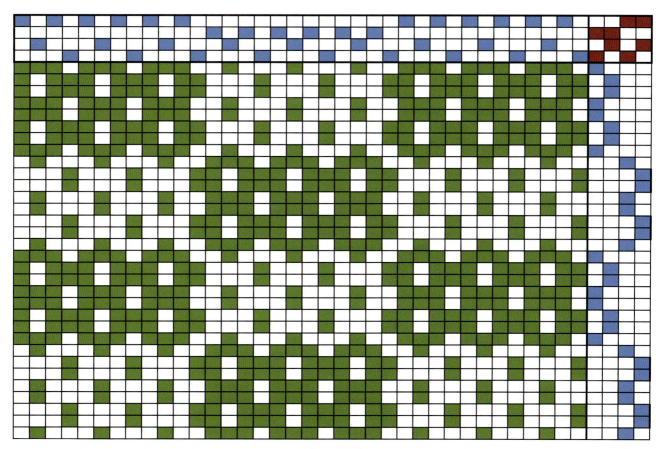

Figure 1.11

SUMMER AND WINTER | 7

Figure 1.13

The last treadling sequence is columns, also known as *dukagång*. In Figure 1.14, you see that you raise one shaft as many times as desired for your design. If you have more than four, you will still choose one column.

This treadling sequence has a very unique and recognizable design (Figure 1.15). There is no particular time to use this treadling pattern. It is strictly a design choice.

Computer programs are wonderful for helping you to decide which treadling sequence to use. If you are weaving circles or want a softer corner, the O's pattern works best. But if you want a blocky look with a sharp corner, use the X's. When I am designing, I will put all four sequences into my computer program to help me decide which one I want to use.

Remember that when using a computer program, you will often see what looks like long warp floats. Remember that you will be using a tabby after each pattern thread, which will eliminate the floats.

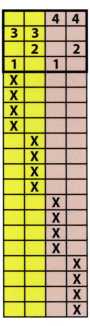

Figure 1.14 Columns, or *dukagång*, treadling sequence.

8 | SUMMER AND WINTER

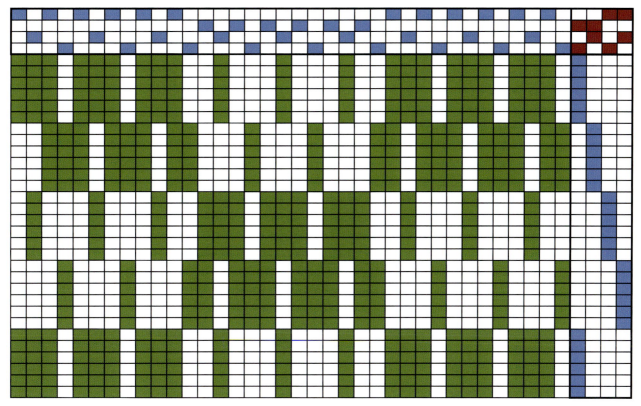

Figure 1.15

Summer and Winter Tie-ups

The tie-up for any weaving graph can be a stumbling block for many weavers. We often just use what is given without any understanding of why it is set up the way it is. However, summer and winter has a specific arrangement for the tie-up. Once you understand it, you will see that it is really very simple. There will be some repetition in this section, so bear with me.

Remember that shafts 1 and 2 are your tie-down shafts. Shafts 3 through 8 are your pattern shafts. Every pattern thread has to be connected to a tie-down thread. This method uses 2 treadles for each pattern thread. We will be looking at a very basic tie-up.

We will begin with 4 shafts. Remember that there are specific treadling sequences for summer and winter: columns (*dukagång*), O's, X's, and alternating. For demonstration purposes, I will work with just the O's method. Figure 1.16 shows a graph of O's treadling.

Figure 1.16 O's treadling.

In order to complete one treadling sequence, remember that it involves two columns and four throws of the pattern thread and four throws of the tabby thread.

Figure 1.17 shows the 4-shaft tie-up. Note that shaft 3 is coupled with shaft 1, and then shaft 3 is coupled with shaft 2. This arrangement is repeated for shaft 4. You can see this approach in the first four columns of the tie-up. Next, let's see what makes up the tabby tie-up. Remember that shafts 1 and 2 are the first set of tabby threads, so that leaves shafts 3 and 4 as the second set of tabby threads for a 4-shaft loom. You can see this in the last two columns in Figure 1.17.

			T	T	
		4	4		4
3	3				3
		2		2	
1		1		1	

Figure 1.17 Tie-up for a 4-shaft loom.

SUMMER AND WINTER | 9

Now let's put the tie-up and the treadling together (Figure 1.18).

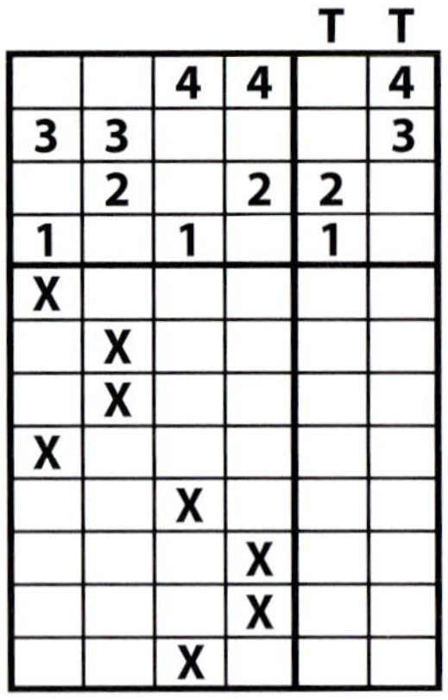

Figure 1.18

What you need to see here is the relationship between the treadling sequence and the tie-up. When treadle 1 is depressed, it raises shafts 1 and 3 (Figure 1.19).

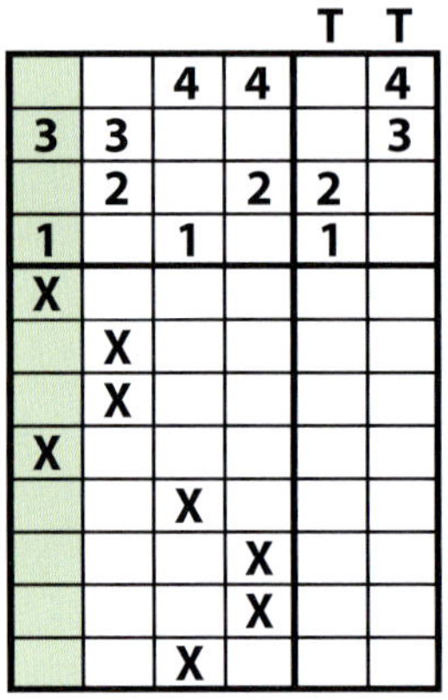

Figure 1.19

When treadle 2 is depressed, it raises shafts 2 and 3 (Figure 1.20).

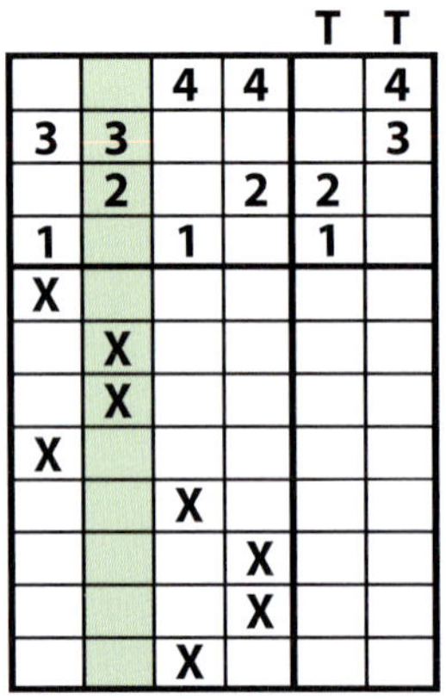

Figure 1.20

Those two treadles complete one-half of the O's treadling sequence. The treadling sequence will be completed by depressing treadle 2 again and finishing with treadle 1. Figure 1.21 shows the first completed treadling. Remember that there are four parts to this treadling sequence.

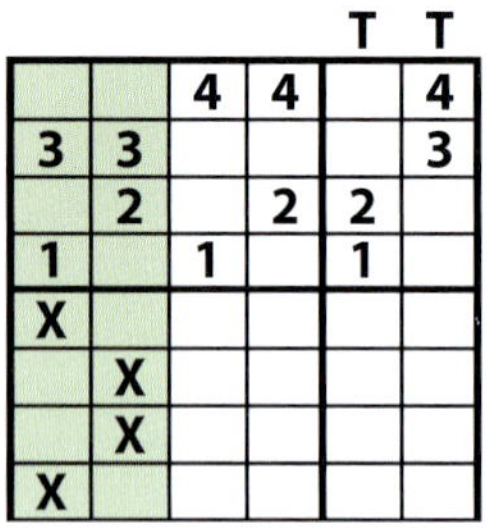

Figure 1.21

Moving on to the second part of the treadling sequence: When treadle 3 is depressed, it raises shafts 1 and 4 (Figure 1.22).

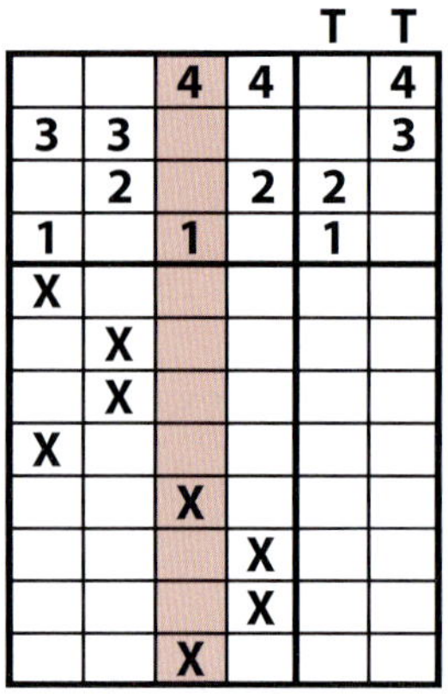

Figure 1.22

When treadle 4 is depressed, it raises shafts 2 and 4 (Figure 1.23).

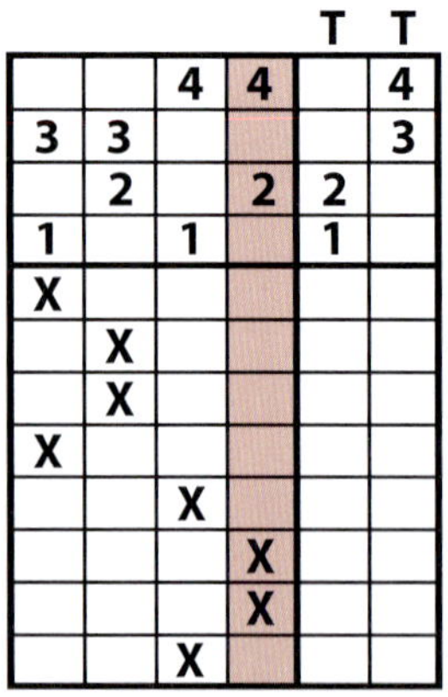

Figure 1.23

10 | SUMMER AND WINTER

These two treadles complete one-half of the O's treadling sequence. To finish the O's pattern sequence, treadle 4 will be repeated, followed by treadle 3. The full treadling sequence is shown in Figure 1.24. Again, all four components must be done before the O's treadling sequence is complete.

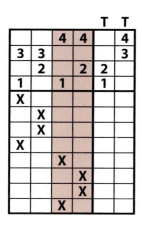

Figure 1.24

Remember, every pattern shaft must be separately connected to both a 1 and a 2 tie-down shaft. Shafts 1 and 2 are tie-down shafts. Shafts 3 and 4 are the pattern shafts for a 4-shaft loom, and shafts 3 through 8 are pattern shafts for an 8-shaft loom. Figure 1.25 shows a 4-shaft tie-up with an O's treadling pattern.

Figure 1.25 A 4-shaft tie-up with an O's treadling pattern.

When you are treadling summer and winter in either O's or X's treadling sequence, you should complete all four steps. With alternating treadling and columnar treadling, you have more flexibility. The object is to have a well-balanced motif! And don't forget to add the tabby after each pattern thread!

Now on to 8 shafts! The tie-up for 8 shafts follows the same principle as for 4—there are just more shafts. Figure 1.26 shows a very basic 8-shaft tie-up for summer and winter.

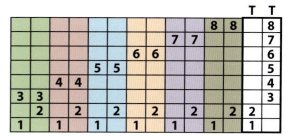

Figure 1.26 A basic 8-shaft tie-up for summer and winter.

Each block has been color-coded to show you that each pattern shaft is separately connected to either the 1 or the 2 tie-down shaft. The treadling sequence that you choose makes no difference at this point. Just be sure to complete the sequence.

Ah, but here is the problem: Looking at the tie-up, you can see that you would have to have 14 treadles. Eight-shaft looms have only 10 treadles!

Tie-ups are usually even more complex than this one. Working with more than 4 shafts allows you to get many more patterns and images, which makes the tie-up more complex. And there is often more than one shaft tied to one treadle. What is the solution?

Figure 1.27 shows the original tie-up for the Shades of Green Scarf (page 111). This was the beginning point in creating this design. It would require 12 treadles to weave this pattern, but I have only 10.

Figure 1.27 The original tie-up for the Shades of Green Scarf would have required 12 treadles.

SUMMER AND WINTER | 11

Look at the final tie-up for the Shades of Green Scarf (Figure 1.28). This is called a "skeleton" tie-up. The final tie-up needs only 10 treadles, which is what I have with an 8-shaft loom. So how was the second tie-up created? There is a wonderful free program, Tim's Treadle Reducer, into which you can put the original tie-up, and it will create a tie-up that will work for *your* jack loom.

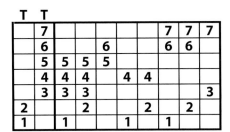

Figure 1.28 The final tie-up for the Shades of Green Scarf.

Tim's Treadle Reducer
(https://www.cs.earlham.edu/~timm/treadle/)

This program creates these skeleton tie-ups, and it is very easy to use. Follow the instructions on the site and you will have a new tie-up—if it is possible. There have been occasions when the program was unable to create a skeleton tie-up from my input. This result takes me back to square one to do some redesigning. *Be sure to include the required tabby when working with this program.*

As you have probably noticed in the projects, when a skeleton tie-up is created, you will often have to do *multi-pedal* treadling—in other words, depressing more than one treadle at a time. In the tie-up above, the tabby was still as it should be; however, there may be times when the tabby will be a combination of two different treadles. You will see multi-pedaling often in the projects in this book. The next chapter explains in more detail how multi-pedal treadling works.

CHAPTER

2 Multi-Pedal Treadling for a Jack Loom

Let's talk about multi-pedal treadling and why it is necessary. We often think that the only time we would depress two treadles at the same time is when we have a direct tie-up loom. But that is not always the case. We will compare the original Shades of Green Scarf tie-up (Figure 2.1) with the skeleton tie-up (Figure 2.2) to examine multi-pedal treadling.

T	T										
	7					7	7	7	7	7	7
	6			6	6	6	6	6	6		
	5	5	5	5	5		5				
	4	4	4	4	4	5				4	4
	3	3	3					3	3	3	3
2			2		2		2		2		2
1		1		1		1		1		1	

Figure 2.1 Original Shades of Green Scarf tie-up.

T	T								
	7						7	7	7
	6			6			6	6	6
	5	5	5	5					
	4	4	4		4	4			
	3	3	3						3
2			2			2		2	
1		1			1		1		

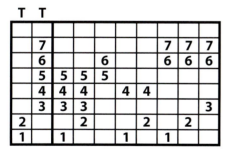

Figure 2.2 Skeleton tie-up for Shades of Green Scarf.

The original tie-up for Shades of Green uses 12 treadles. An 8-shaft loom has only 10 treadles, so this tie-up simply won't work. Using Tim's Treadle Reducer, we created a tie-up that is usable, but only with multi-pedal treadling.

To break this concept down to help you understand, I've isolated one set of the tie-up. In order to create the summer and winter motif/pattern, we will need to raise shafts 1, 4, 5, 6 together and then 2, 4, 5, 6 together. These are highlighted in Figure 2.3, which is the original tie-up. Remember this point as we go forward.

T	T										
	7					7	7	7	7	7	7
	6			6	6	6	6	6	6		
	5	5	5	5	5		5				
	4	4	4	4	4	5				4	4
	3	3	3					3	3	3	3
2			2		2		2		2		2
1		1		1		1		1		1	

Figure 2.3

Now we will break down the multi-pedal treadling in detail. Figure 2.4 shows the Shades of Green Scarf skeleton tie-up with just a partial treadling sequence. The treadling has been highlighted with an arrow and pink blocks. If you follow the first line of X's to the tie-up, you will see that when you depress the first treadle, you are raising shafts 5 and 6. The second treadle raises 1 and 4. By depressing these treadles together, you are raising 1, 4, 5, and 6. Look back at the original tie-up with highlights (Figure 2.3), and you will see that you have accomplished just what is needed.

Now we will move to the second part of the pattern. In Figure 2.5, when you depress the first highlighted treadle, you are raising shafts 5 and 6. When depressing the second treadle, you are raising shafts 2 and 4. By depressing them together, you are raising shafts 2, 4, 5, and 6. Looking at the original tie-up with highlights

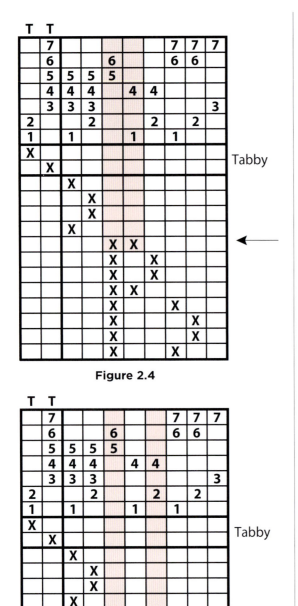

Figure 2.4

Figure 2.5

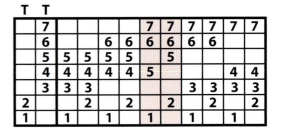

Figure 2.6 Original tie-up.

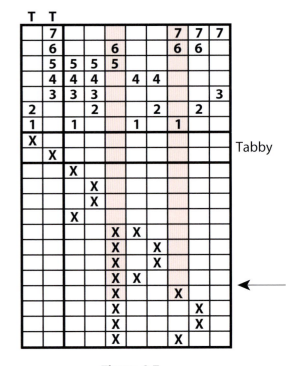

Figure 2.7

(Figure 2.3), you can see that you have accomplished the second half of the pattern. Remember the rules of summer and winter: each set of pattern shafts must include shaft 1 followed by the same set including shaft 2. Multi-pedal treadling has made this possible.

Let's look at another example. In the original tie-up with highlights shown in Figure 2.6, you will need to raise shafts 1, 5, 6, 7, followed by shafts 2, 5, 6, 7. This step is accomplished in Figure 2.7. If you look at the line indicated by the arrow and the pink column up to the tie-up, you can see that with one treadle, you are raising shafts 5 and 6, and with the other treadle, you are raising 1, 6, and 7. Shaft 6 is raised by both treadles. That is not a problem, so don't let it throw you. This outcome is not unusual in skeleton tie-ups. The main thing is that using these two treadles together raises shafts 1, 5, 6, 7, which is exactly what you needed.

Now we move on to create the second half of the pattern. In Figure 2.8, the arrow lines up with the next pair of treadles. Follow the pink columns up to the tie-up, and you will see that one treadle raises shafts 5 and 6 and the second treadle now raises shafts 2, 6, and 7. Again there is an overlap of shaft 6. But once again you have raised shafts 2, 5, 6, and 7, which is what you needed to accomplish.

14 | MULTI-PEDAL TREADLING FOR A JACK LOOM

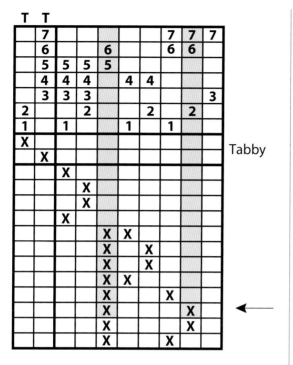

Figure 2.8

Multi-pedal treadling is very common in summer and winter, especially as the motifs and tie-ups become more complex. Just be sure to carefully read the treadling so you know where it is indicated.

There is one more very important detail to remember about skeleton tie-ups and multi-pedal treadling. When you have used Tim's Treadle Reducer to create a new tie-up, don't forget that you will have to redesign the treadling sequence. This program will tell you what treadles need to be combined. I use Fiberworks Bronze in my designing, so I will create a new image with the original threading sequence and the skeleton tie-up. Then, following the instructions in Tim's Treadle Reducer, I will put in the new treadling sequence. This approach allows me to make sure that I've followed the instructions correctly and have the same image/motif that was created with the original tie-up.

MULTI-PEDAL TREADLING FOR A JACK LOOM | 15

Profile Drafts

When I was learning to weave, I frequently heard the term "profile draft." It took me a while to get my head around what this was, to understand what it meant and how to use it. It is often assumed that everyone knows what a profile draft is, but I've found that isn't the case. Since profile drafting is a very important part of summer and winter, I want to explain what it means and how to use it.

Profile Threading

The easiest definition for a profile draft is that it is a form of shorthand for weavers. Instead of writing out a threading draft in full, blocks that are lettered or darkened are used to indicate a *set* of threads. Figure 3.1 shows the two threading blocks used for 4-shaft summer and winter. We will refer to them as Block A and Block B.

Profile drafts are most often written in the two ways shown in Figure 3.2. These profile drafts mean exactly the same thing: three Block A's and three Block B's.

In a profile draft, the blocks in Figure 3.1 are substituted into the profile draft. Where there was an A, the threading in A block is substituted. Where there was a B, the threading in B block is substituted. Figure 3.3 shows

Figure 3.1 Blocks A and B for 4-shaft summer and winter.

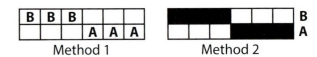

Figure 3.2 Both of these profile drafts indicate three A blocks and three B blocks.

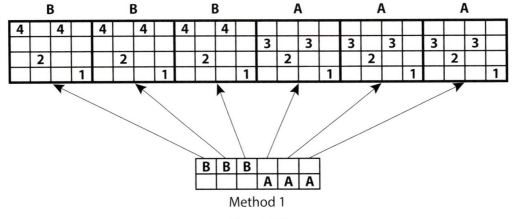

Figure 3.3

16 | PROFILE DRAFTS

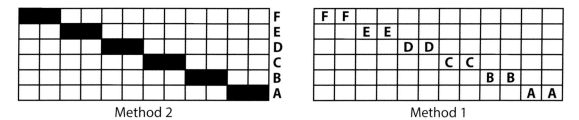

Figure 3.4 Two ways to write an 8-shaft profile draft.

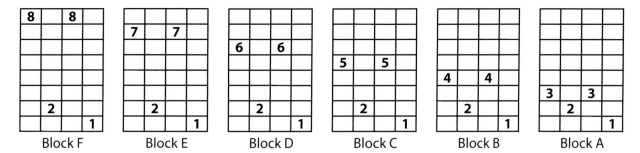

Figure 3.5 Threading blocks for 8-shaft summer and winter.

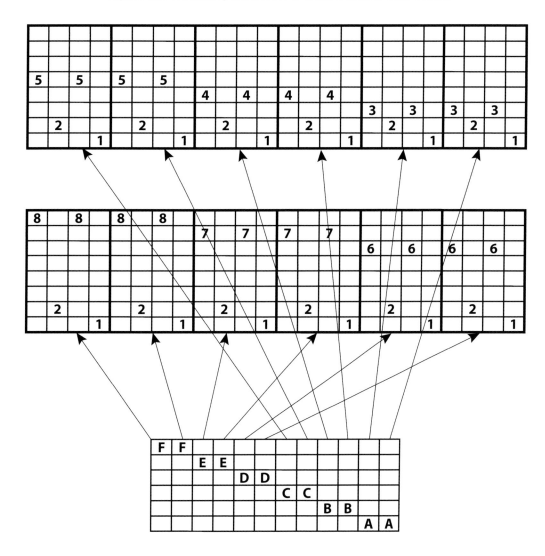

Figure 3.6 Profile draft showing the threading blocks substituted.

PROFILE DRAFTS | 17

how these summer and winter blocks are substituted for the blocks in the profile draft. This graph shows the threading written out in full. You can see that the shorthand of profile drafts is a huge space saver.

Now let's look at 8 shafts. Figure 3.4 shows the 8-shaft profile draft written in the two different options.

Next are the threading pattern blocks for 8-shaft summer and winter (Figure 3.5). Once again, where there is an A block, the 4-thread A block is substituted. Where there is a B block, the 4-thread B block is substituted, and so on. Figure 3.6 shows these substitutions.

The first thing you should notice is that the full threading draft had to be put on two separate lines because it is so long. Working with large threading drafts can become very cumbersome, which is why profile drafts are so convenient. However, when you are threading your loom, if you still find the profile draft confusing, feel free to use graph paper to write out the draft in full. I will often do this when using a profile draft. Nothing to be embarrassed about! Make it easy for you!

Profile Treadling

Is there such a thing as profile drafts for treadling? Of course! Some weave structures have specific treadling sequences, and this is the case with summer and winter. There are four basic treadling sequences associated with summer and winter. Figure 3.7 shows these sequences written out in full. You can look back at Figure 1.10 on page 7 to see their relationship to the tie-up.

Except in the case of columns (*dukagång*) and singles, treadling for summer and winter is done in pairs.

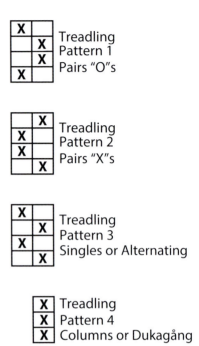

Figure 3.7 The four basic treadling sequences for summer and winter.

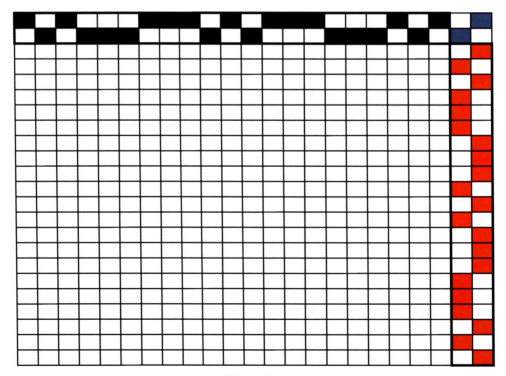

Figure 3.8

18 | PROFILE DRAFTS

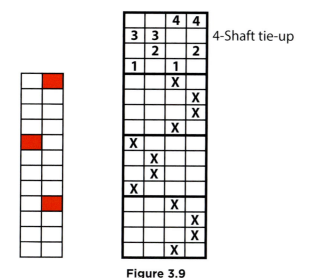

Figure 3.9

In Figure 3.8, the profile treadling pattern blocks have been indicated in red.

One of the treadling patterns in Figure 3.7 is then substituted for each red square. To help you understand, in Figure 3.9 I have written out the first three blocks of the treadling graph using treadling pattern 1, Pairs O's.

Any of the pattern blocks can be substituted for each red square or letter. It makes no difference if you are doing 4 shafts or more. If you are working with an 8-shaft loom, the process remains the same. Choose one treadling pattern and substitute the four threads for one red block. In the case of patterns 3 or 4, you can repeat the treadling pattern as desired for your project. When I start treadling, I usually write out the treadling pattern in full, as I find that easier to follow. And always remember to add the tabby! It is generally not included in the treadling pattern but is indicated in the instructions or at the side of the treadling sequence.

Profile drafts should not be confusing. They are just a method to condense the information into a more concise form.

Profile Tie-ups

We have looked at profile threading and profile treadling. What about the tie-up? Tie-ups always depend on the weave structure you have chosen to use. It will be different for summer and winter, Quigley, or twill. A profile tie-up is unusual, but it is possible that you may come across one. *8-Shaft Patterns* by Carol Strickler uses profile tie-ups in the section on summer and winter. We will look at just one (Figure 3.10).

Figure 3.10 Example of a profile tie-up from *8-Shaft Patterns* by Carol Strickler.

Looking at this profile tie-up as is makes absolutely no sense. But there are full tie-ups included in the book. Sometimes they are beside the profile draft, but know that they will be on the same page. It is important that you have some familiarity with summer and winter to fully understand the tie-up. But moving forward, the full threading in the Strickler book is written out as in Figure 3.11. The appropriate tie-up blocks have been used instead of the lettered blocks. I put the letters above the tie-up so you can see the relationship.

Figure 3.11 The full tie-up.

The "a" and "b" indicate your tabby tie-up shafts. If you compare the tie-ups in Figures 3.10 and 3.11, they mean the same thing, but Figure 3.11 is the *full* tie-up. The difference in the tie-ups with the same letter is the

PROFILE DRAFTS | 19

use of either shaft 1 *or* shaft 2. Remember your basics . . . every summer and winter pattern shaft has to be connected to shaft 1 and then shaft 2 on sequential treadles. Look at Figure 3.12, in which one set of shafts has been isolated. Shafts 3 through 7 are used for both treadles. The only difference is one column includes shaft 1 and the other column includes shaft 2. This is a consistent feature in all summer and winter treadling.

Look at Figure 3.11 again, and you will immediately realize that an 8-shaft loom has only 10 treadles and this tie-up uses 14 treadles. Not to worry! Remember earlier I told you about Tim's Treadle Reducer. Put this chart into the program, and it will reduce to a usable tie-up. Then you will need to adjust the treadling pattern, and you will also be multi-pedal treadling. This is where a computer program is a huge help. You can put all of the information into your program and verify that you have made all of the changes correctly. With the tie-ups in the Strickler book, you will have to work through this process each time.

Designing with Profile Drafts

Profile drafts are also wonderful for designing! Let's look at a simple profile threading draft again (Figure 3.13).

Remember that each threading block represents *4 threads*! If you were to write this graph out fully with all of the threads, it would be huge. The threading graph would have 92 threads (4 × 23 = 92)!

Next, add the tie-up and treadling! This draft is trompe as writ, or treadled as threaded, so the next step is to fill in the drawdown (Figure 3.14). Of course, you are designing, so you can change this if you want.

And the draft is complete (Figure 3.15)! This draft gives you a good visual on how the pattern will look when woven. Profile drafts allow you to try all different ideas in threading and treadling without having to put in all of the individual threads. Once you decide on your pattern, you can create a full draft. Then you can try the different treadling patterns to see which you like best. If you work with a computer program, it can make designing with profile drafts very easy and fun.

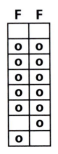

Figure 3.12

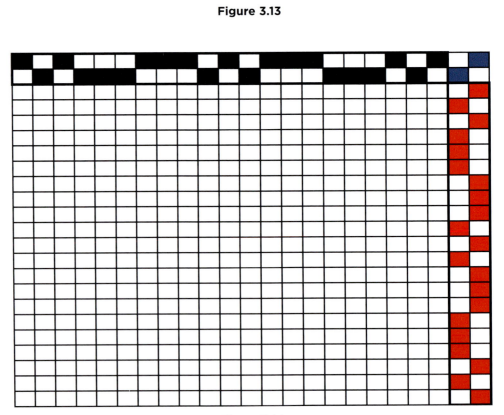

Figure 3.13

Figure 3.14

20 | PROFILE DRAFTS

What about 8-shaft patterns? Approach them in exactly the same way, except now you will have more pattern shafts. Look at Figure 3.16 and see how using profiles to design gives you a preview of your design.

In this graph, you can see the threading, treadling, and full drawdown of the pattern. This tie-up is the very simplest form of tie-up. Don't look at the drawdown and think you are seeing long floats. *Remember that this is a profile draft.* This is just a design profile draft to see whether you like the overall look or want to try more options. Designing with profile drafts is easy and fun, and it really allows you to see many different options.

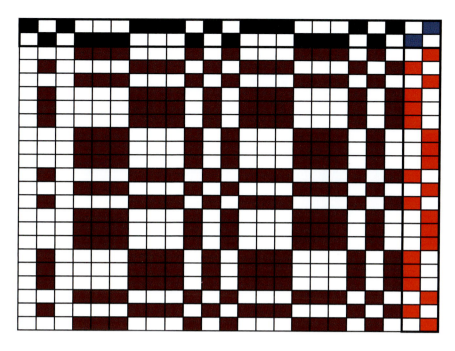

Figure 3.15

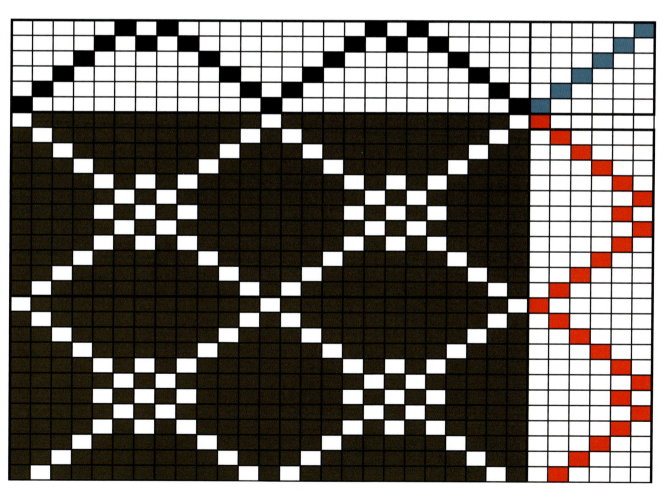

Figure 3.16

PROFILE DRAFTS | 21

CHAPTER 4

Fiber and Color

Many of the original summer and winter coverlets have a cotton warp and wool pattern thread. These pieces are wonderful! But contemporary weavers have so many options in fiber choice and are not limited to just cotton and wool: unmercerized cotton, mercerized/perle cotton, silks, Tencel, and wool! And we can use any of these when weaving summer and winter. So, unless you are re-creating an old piece, think outside the box and use something new.

Many of the projects in this book use perle cotton. Perle cotton is available through many sources and in many colors, and it is affordable. It is the perfect choice for scarves, shawls, and other projects. Lunatic Fringe offers an incredible range of colors based on the color wheel, which is loads of fun to work with. Crabapple Yarns hand dyes perle cotton and creates multiple variegated colorways. Always look to indie dyers! I love the fiber dyed by Aisling Yarns (https://www.aislingyarns.com/) for both color and quality. There are many indie dyers who are creating new colorways. And many of these dyers will do custom blends just for you.

For dishtowels and hand towels, I use both mercerized and unmercerized cotton. Unmercerized cotton is more absorbent, but the colors are often more muted. If I'm looking for very vibrant colors, I will choose mercerized cotton. Over time these towels will become more absorbent, so do not worry.

Tencel is a wonderful fiber for shawls and scarves and is affordable. Tencel comes in many colors, so you have a lot of choices. Do an internet search! A favorite indie dyer of mine, Shiny Dime Fibers (https://www.shinydimefibers.com/), hand dyes Tencel to create new and different variegated colorways that are fun and unique.

One note on Tencel: When weaving summer and winter, you will always use a floating selvedge. Use two strands of Tencel on each side of your project, as Tencel floating selvedges tend to break. The use of two threads will help to prevent this.

Summer and winter projects normally use two different sizes of thread. The pattern thread is two times the size of the warp and tabby thread. So, if you are using 10/2 for the warp, you would use 5/2 or a similar size for the pattern thread. The tabby thread is normally the same thread as the warp, although it could be smaller. You could choose to use 20/2 instead of 10/2. Read on, though . . . you will see that I often break these rules!

You can use multiple colors in the warp in different ways. Create stripes in bold, different colors or colors that are side by side on the color wheel. The Autumn Splendor Placemat and Napkins (page 27) are an example of this technique. This set of placemats uses three different colors in the warp.

You can use a variegated color fiber for the warp. Then, for the pattern thread, you have a choice. Use one of the dominant colors in the variegated thread or go with another totally different color for contrast. The Purple Haze Scarf (page 33) is an example of this technique, using one of the Crabapple yarns.

Another warp idea is a stash buster. We all have those partial cones with anywhere from 10 yards or more. And we just can't bear to throw them away. Pull them out and line them up on the table. Using your McMorran balance, estimate how much yardage each cone has. Do you have enough for your chosen project? If you have plenty of options, decide which ones look good together and which ones to set aside for another

22 | FIBER AND COLOR

time. Winding the warp can be fussy. You don't want to create stripes, but rather a random placement of the colors. There are many ways to achieve this result, and it also depends on whether you dress your loom from front to back or back to front. I dress my loom from front to back, which means I sley the reed before I thread the heddles. This approach allows me to easily place my colors in the reed in a random manner. The Blue Cubed Table Runner (page 59) and the Sunspots Table Runner (page 113) are two projects using this technique.

Summer and winter also uses a tabby thread—another area where you can play with color. I love to use one color in the warp and a second color for the tabby. Doing so will often give the background an iridescent effect. This technique was used in the Lace Runner (page 91) project.

You can also change the tabby with each motif. Use a white/neutral thread for the warp and one color for the pattern thread. For the tabby thread, use pastels to create a spring project. Or use soft browns and rusts, and you will have an autumn project. How about red and green tabbies for a Christmas project? Look at the Color Play Placemat (page 79) for an example of this technique. In this project, I used four colors of 10/2 for the warp and four colors of 10/2 for the tabby.

Now let's look at the Shades of Green Scarf. The warp thread is 10/2 perle cotton in Bali, which is a bright green. The pattern thread is 5/2 white perle cotton. But the tabby—here is something different! I used 20/2 perle cotton from Lunatic Fringe in analogous green colors. Now this project became a 3-shuttle weave. I lined up the colors as they would appear on the color wheel, dark to light, and wound a bobbin of each. Keeping the bobbins in order, I wove the first pattern thread, and then I created the tabby by one pass of color one followed by another pass of color two in the same shed. This process was repeated for the first motif. When I got to the second motif, I changed out color one for color three and wove the second motif. I used five different colors of 20/2 perle cotton and worked my way through a combination of each color and then reversed back to the original two colors. This was a fussy process, but the effect is a very soft change of the green background. I used the green palette, but any color palette could be used.

Play with color, use your imagination, and, most important, think outside the box! Trying something different is always fun.

Now, back to breaking some rules. As I said before, the pattern thread is normally twice the size of the warp and tabby thread. But as I was weaving projects, there were times when I would choose not to do this. It might have been a color choice or simply wanting to use what I had on hand. What happens if you use the same size thread for both warp and weft? Absolutely nothing—it works! You will still see the motif just fine, and the overall look is more delicate.

Doubling a Smaller Thread to Use as a Pattern Thread

If you do want a larger thread for your pattern and you have the correct color in 10/2 but not 5/2, how do you double this thread in an easy manner? Or, if you want to make sure you are using the same color for the pattern that you have used in a warp stripe but in a thicker size, what should you do? You have three options.

One option is to use a shuttle that holds two bobbins. But not everyone owns one of these. Another option is to wind one bobbin with your color. Then, holding that bobbin and a thread from the cone, wind these two threads onto another bobbin, thus doubling the size of the fiber. I find this process problematic. It is very difficult to get the two threads to wind evenly; one always ends up being a bit longer, and it gets fussy at the edges.

The next option is my favorite. Because you are using a floating selvedge, you can easily double the thread while weaving. Wind your bobbin with the 10/2 thread in your color choice. Create the shed for the first pattern thread and throw the shuttle, and then beat. *Open that same shed a second time* and throw the shuttle again and then beat. Now you have placed two 10/2 threads in the same shed and essentially created a 5/2 thread. Because these have been placed separately, you don't have to fuss with the selvedge as you would with either of the other options.

Summer and winter is a wonderful weave that gives you so many options to play with color and fiber choices. If you are unsure of your initial decisions, just add a bit to your warp before you begin your project and try some different fibers and colors. Have fun!

FIBER AND COLOR | 23

4-SHAFT PROJECTS

The key below is for substituting blocks into the threading drafts. Substitute all four threads for each lettered block in the project charts. Remember that when you have only 4 shafts, you are limited to 2 pattern threads.

Key to Block A and Block B for 4-shaft projects

Autumn Splendor Placemat and Napkins

This set of placemats and napkins will be perfect for Thanksgiving dinner with the family. This may be just a set of four, but you can easily increase the warp and make more to fit the size of your family. Another option would be to weave a long table runner and then make multiple napkins. So many ideas!

Begin and end each piece with plain weave and hem stitching. I left a narrow fringe on each piece. If you have a serger, you could easily serge the edges of the napkins for a different finish.

Now to the color! The color in the warp is set, but you get to play in the weft/tabby colors. The main pattern color is the Avocado perle cotton. But the tabby color changes with each block. In the treadling, Motif A uses the 10/2 Flaxon. But when you weave Motif B, you will alternate using the 10/2 California Gold and 10/2 Lunatic Fringe Copper. When you weave the napkins, you will follow this color arrangement but won't have a pattern thread. A word of caution: I found that it was easy to make a treadling mistake and not see it from the front of the piece. To help catch mistakes on the underside, I used a hand mirror. After I finished a block, I held the hand mirror on the underside so I could see any errors. Best to find them quickly!

Make this set your own by changing colors. You could increase or decrease the number of different colors to suit your home.

Dimensions: Placemats, 12 inches × 15.5 inches (30.5 × 39.25 cm); Napkins, 12 inches × 12 inches (30.5 × 30.5 cm)

Warp
Sett: 24 epi, 12 dent reed, 2 threads per dent
Length: 5-yard (4.6-m) warp
Threads: 10/2 perle cotton
- Flaxon: 80 ends plus 2 floating selvedges = 82 ends, 425 yards (388.6 m)
- California Gold: 96 ends, 500 yards (457.2 m)
- Copper by Lunatic Fringe: 120 ends, 625 yards (571.5 m)

Weft
5/2 perle cotton
- Avocado: 450 yards (411.5 m)

Tabby: 10/2 perle cotton
- Flaxon: 180 yards (164.6 m)
- California Gold: 320 yards (292.6 m)
- Copper by Lunatic Fringe: 400 yards (365.8 m)

Note: The tabby color changes throughout this pattern

Threading
Full Motif: 4 times
Partial Motif: 1 time

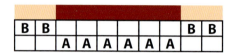

Partial Motif
40 ends

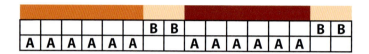

Full Motif
64 ends

Treadling
Alternate Motifs A and B: 11 times
End with Motif A.
Add tabby after each pattern thread.
Refer to text for color changes and instructions for napkins.

Footpath Table Runner

A solitary walk in the woods can be just what you need to brighten your day and put all the problems in perspective. This table runner reminds me of those walks: appreciating different colors of leaves, that special smell of autumn, and the occasional sparkle of birch bark. Not crazy about the brown palette? Change to greens or blues! You could even make each warp repeat a different color, which would make a lovely striped runner.

Begin and end this piece with 0.5 inches (1.25 cm) of plain weave and hem stitching. If you prefer, you can do 2 inches (5.1 cm) of plain weave and finish with a rolled hem.

Dimensions: 15.5 inches × 50 inches (39.25 × 127 cm)

Warp
Sett: 24 epi, 12 dent reed, 2 threads per dent
Length: 3-yard (2.7-m) warp
Threads: 10/2 perle cotton
- Natural: 36 ends plus 2 floating selvedges = 38 ends, 125 yards (114.3 m)
- Oak: 336 ends, 1,025 yards (937.3 m)

Weft
5/2 perle cotton, Brown: 500 yards (457.2 m)
Tabby: 10/2 perle cotton
- Natural: 50 yards (45.7 m)
- Oak: 450 yards (411.5 m)

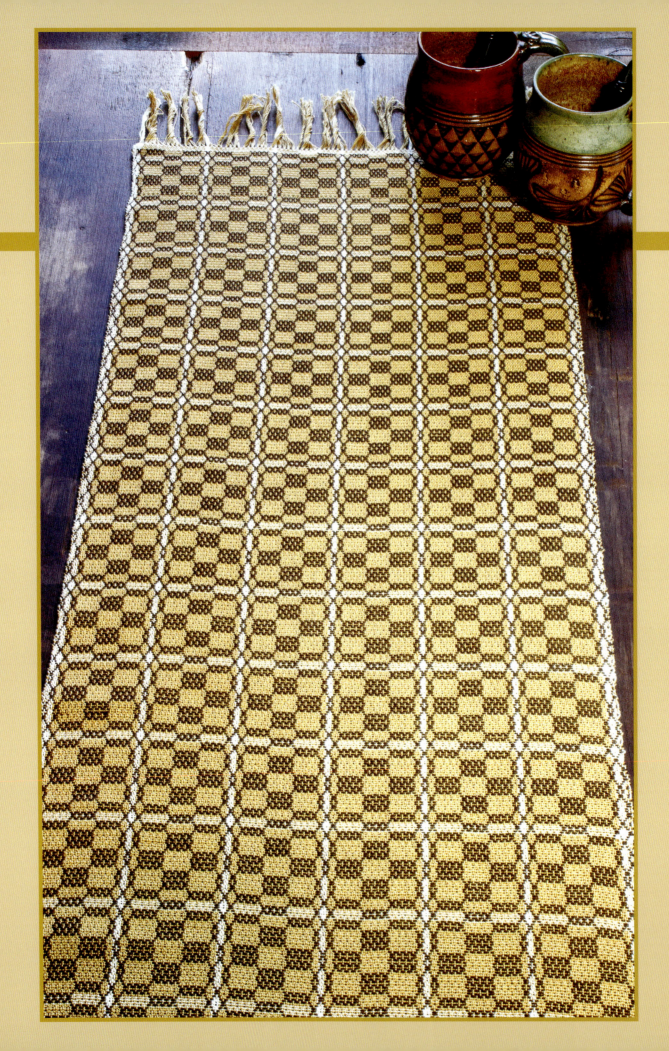

Threading
Border 1: 1 time
Motif: 6 times
Border 2: 1 time

Border 2
8 ends

Motif
60 ends

Border 1
4 ends

Treadling
Alternate Motifs A and B to desired length.
End with Motif A.
Note the repeats within Motif B.
Color indicates tabby thread! Pattern thread is brown.

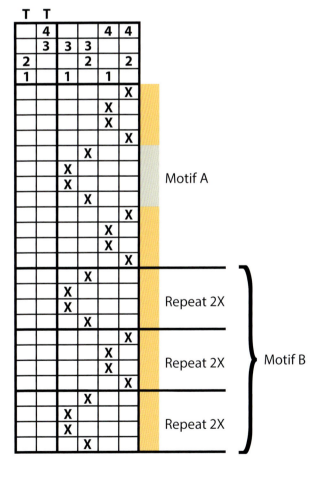

FOOTPATH TABLE RUNNER | 31

Purple Haze Scarf

Finding a variegated 10/2 cotton is a treat! Crabapple Yarns makes just that, and it is available through Red Stone Glen in Pennsylvania. There are many different colorways to choose from. And the variety of solid colors from Lunatic Fringe makes matching colors oh so easy! I chose to go with a dark purple but just as easily could have chosen blue or violet for the pattern thread. Be sure to check out these fibers and add them to your stash. You will see other projects in this book using different colorways from Crabapple. The hardest part is choosing which to use for your project!

Begin and end this project with 0.5 inches (1.25 cm) of plain weave and hem stitching.

Dimensions: 7 inches × 62 inches, plus 4-inch fringe
(17.75 × 157.5 cm, 10.25-cm fringe)

Warp
Sett: 24 epi, 12 dent reed, 2 threads per dent
Length: 3-yard (2.7-m) warp
Thread: 10/2 perle cotton, Piñata by Crabapple Yarns: 168 ends plus 2 floating selvedges = 170 ends, 550 yards (502.9 m)

Weft
5/2 perle cotton by Lunatic Fringe: 5 Purple, 300 yards (274.3 m)
Tabby: 10/2 perle cotton, Orchid by Crabapple Yarns: 300 yards (274.3 m)

Threading
Full Motif: 3 times
Partial Motif: 1 time

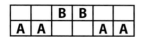

Partial Motif
24 ends

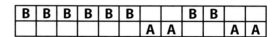

Full Motif
48 ends

Treadling
Full Motif: 41 times or to desired length
End with Partial Motif to balance.
Add tabby after each pattern thread.

Full Motif

Partial Motif

Sea Glass Table Runner

My friend Amy has a summer house on a lake and often shares pictures of the sea glass that she collects over the summer. Sea glass is weathered broken glass from bottles and glassware. I've always been fascinated with the different blues and greens that she finds. And, of course, I'm partial to those colors. When I was looking through my fiber supply, there were some colors that just made me think of sea glass. So naturally I had to make a runner in that color palette. I used three different colors in the warp, alternating them but not concerned that I began and ended with the same color. Feel free to add more colors or just work with two colors. Below is the color sequence, each having 16 threads:

- Sea Green – Sky Blue – Teal

There are a total of 8 Teal stripes, 8 Sky Blue stripes, and 7 Sea Green stripes. Begin and end the runner with 0.5 inches (1.25 cm) of plain weave, hem stitching, and fringe. If you prefer, weave 1.5 inches (3.75 cm) of plain weave and finish with a rolled hem.

Dimensions: 15 inches × 48 inches, plus 3-inch fringe (38 × 122 cm, 7.5-cm fringe)

Warp
Sett: 24 epi, 12 dent reed, 2 threads per dent
Length: 2.5-yard (2.3-m) warp
Threads: 10/2 perle cotton
- Teal by Lunatic Fringe: 128 ends, 350 yards (320 m)
- Sky Blue by Lunatic Fringe: 128 ends, 350 yards (320 m)
- Sea Green by Lunatic Fringe: 112 ends, 300 yards (274.3 m)

Note: You will need a floating selvedge, so be sure to add one thread to the color you begin and end with.

Weft
5/2 perle cotton: 5 Blue Green by Lunatic Fringe, 450 yards (411.5 m)
Tabby: 10/2 Poplin: 450 yards (411.5 m)

Border 1
16 ends

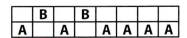

Full Motif
64 ends

Border 2
32 ends

Threading
Border 1: 1 time
Full Motif: 5 times
Border 2: 1 time

Treadling
Alternate Motifs A and B: 27 times
End with Motif A.
Add tabby between each pattern thread.

SEA GLASS TABLE RUNNER | 37

Sherbet Scarf

Summer arrives and there is nothing more refreshing than a bowl of sherbet . . . or wearing this sherbet-colored scarf. Even though the pattern thread is wool, it is light and airy and perfect for a cool morning or evening under the stars. Chroma yarn from KnitPicks has a long color change repeat but stays within the same color family. This quality allows you to see the subtle color change in this scarf. KnitPicks offers other color combinations so you can use this pattern and colors of your choice.

Begin and end with 0.5 inches (1.25 cm) of plain weave and hem stitching.

Dimensions: 7 inches × 64 inches, plus 4-inch fringe
(17.75 × 162.5 cm, 10.25-cm fringe)

Warp
Sett: 24 epi, 12 dent reed, 2 threads per dent
Length: 3-yard (2.7-m) warp
Thread: 10/2 perle cotton, Yellow: 168 ends plus 2 floating selvedges = 170 ends, 550 yards (503 m)

Weft
Chroma Fingering Weight by KnitPicks, Tiki: 396 yards (362.1 m) per skein, 2 skeins
Tabby: 10/2 perle cotton, Yellow: 350 yards (320 m)

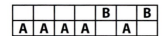

Border 1
28 ends

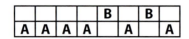

Motif A
32 ends

Motif B
32 ends

Border 2
12 ends

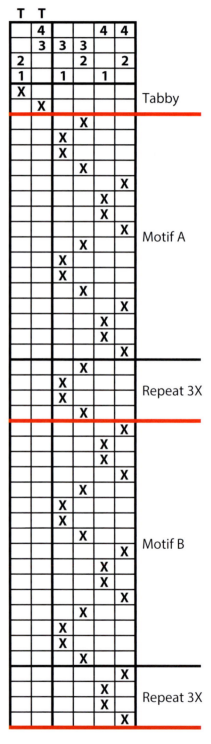

Full Motif

Threading
Border 1: 1 time
Alternate Motifs A and B: 2 times
Border 2: 1 time

Treadling
Alternate Motifs A and B to desired length. End with Motif A. Add tabby between each pattern thread.

40 | SHERBET SCARF

Towels Three Ways

This is the perfect first project to weave in summer and winter and also have three brand new dish towels in the process. Each towel is treadled in a different summer and winter design. You will treadle O's, alternating, and columns. Having treadled each method, not only will you understand the difference, but it will also aid you in future projects to decide which method you like best and which is the best look for your project.

I started and ended each towel with 1.5 inches (3.75 cm) of plain weave, which allows for an ample rolled hem. Be sure to add a tabby thread between each pattern thread. The blocks were treadled to square, but you can be creative and make blocks all different sizes. You could very easily alternate colors in the warp for even fancier towels. After you have woven your first towel, weave 4 passes of a high contrast color to separate your towels. Then you can start weaving the second towel. These are your towels—have fun with them!

Dimensions: 15 inches × 27 inches (38 × 68.5 cm) each

Warp
Sett: 24 epi, 12 dent reed, 2 threads per dent
Length: 4-yard (3.7-m) warp
Thread: 10/2 perle cotton, Natural: 360 ends plus 2 floating selvedges = 362 ends, 1,500 yards (1,371.6 m)

Weft
5/2 perle cotton, Light Rust: 850 yards (777.2 m)
Tabby: 10/2 perle cotton, Natural: 1,000 yards (914.4 m)

Threading
Motif: 7 times
Partial Motif: 1 time

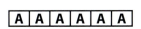

| A | A | A | A | A | A |

Partial Motif
24 ends

| B | B | B | B | B | B | | | | | | |
| | | | | | | A | A | A | A | A | A |

Motif
48 ends

Treadling
For each treadling:
Repeat Motif A to square.
Repeat Motif B to square.
Add tabby between each pattern thread.

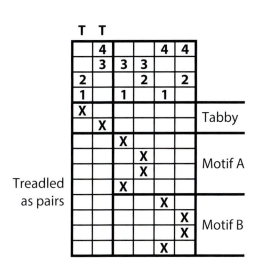

TOWELS THREE WAYS | 43

Tiny Blocks Scarf

Do you want an easy summer and winter piece to start with? This is the one! Since the blocks alternate in both the threading and the treadling, it is easy to accomplish and easy to see the pattern form. And it is also obvious if you've made a mistake and need to correct it. If you wanted to have bigger blocks, you could repeat each motif two times instead of once in both the threading and the treadling. Another idea would be to thread your loom as written but play with the size of the blocks when treadling. You could get an interesting pattern that way.

Notice that in the warp there are two distinctive colors of threads. This adds a bit of interest to your scarf. And it is also a great way to use up those cones of fiber with small amounts. Three colors would be fun to try. Just be sure your pattern thread has enough contrast to stand out.

Begin and end the scarf with plain weave and hem stitching.

Dimensions: 7 inches × 62 inches, plus 3-inch fringe
(17.75 × 157.5 cm, 7.5-cm fringe)

Warp
Sett: 24 epi, 12 dent reed, 2 threads per dent
Length: 3-yard (2.7-m) warp
Threads: 10/2 perle cotton
- Poplin: 88 ends plus 2 floating selvedges = 90 ends, 285 yards (260.6 m)
- Sky Blue by Lunatic Fringe: 80 ends, 285 yards (260.6 m)

Weft
5/2 perle cotton, Black: 275 yards (251.5 m)
Tabby: 10/2 perle cotton, Poplin: 275 yards (251.5 m)

Threading

Alternate Motifs A and B: 10 times

Motif A: 1 time

Motif B
8 ends

Motif A
8 ends

Treadling

Alternate Motifs A and B to desired length.

End with Motif A.

Just for Fun Table Runner

Do you remember this old joke: What is black and white and red all over? A newspaper! But this time the answer is a unique table runner. There are a total of 400 warp threads, 200 in black and 200 in white. I chose to use red for both the pattern thread and the tabby thread. This is such an easy color palette to set up; you could change the colors to reds, oranges, and yellows or blues, greens, and purples. Instead of half and half, you could make four equal stripes. Just use your imagination to create your own extraordinary piece. Reduce the size and make a scarf! There are so many options.

I began and ended with 0.5 inches (1.25 cm) of plain weave and hem stitching. Fringe is optional. You could weave 1.5 inches (3.75 cm) of plain weave and make a rolled hem.

Dimensions: 16.5 inches × 42 inches, plus 3.5-inch fringe
(42 × 106.75 cm, 8.75-cm fringe)

Warp
Sett: 24 epi, 12 dent reed, 2 threads per dent
Length: 2.5-yard (2.3-m) warp
Threads: 10/2 perle cotton
- White: 200 ends plus 1 floating selvedge = 201 ends, 525 yards (480.1 m)
- Black: 200 ends plus 1 floating selvedge = 201 ends, 525 yards (480.1 m)

Weft
5/2 perle cotton, Red: 450 yards (411.5 m)
Tabby: 10/2 perle cotton, Red: 450 yards (411.5 m)

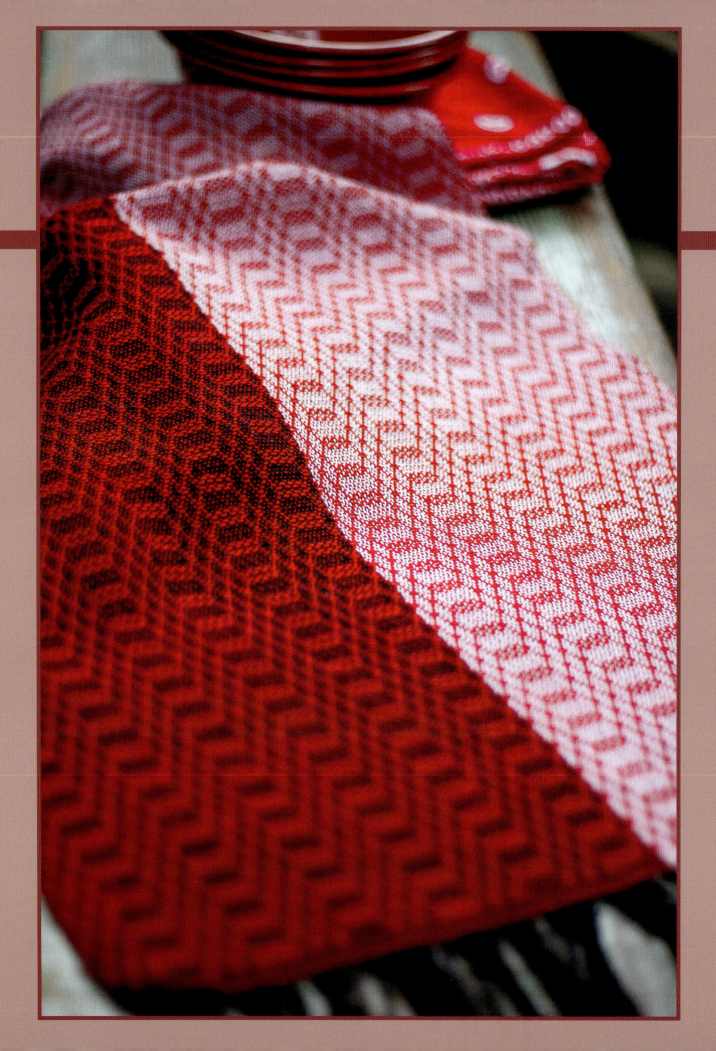

Threading
Full Motif: 6 times
Partial Motif: 1 time

Partial Motif
16 ends

Full Motif
64 ends

Treadling
Alternate Motifs A and B to desired length.
End with Motif A.
Add tabby after each pattern thread.

JUST FOR FUN TABLE RUNNER | 49

Caribbean Nights Shawl

What a lovely shawl to wear on a cool night—ideally on the beach in the Caribbean! The use of Tencel makes this shawl very soft, allowing it to drape beautifully over your shoulders. The Lemongrass color for the weft really gives a sparkle to this piece.

As I began to weave, I decided to put in a group of 6 passes of plain weave between each block. This approach makes the blocks more pronounced. You can leave these out if you prefer.

I used two strands of Tencel on each side of the piece for the floating selvedge. Doing so prevents breakage, which often happens when using Tencel. Begin and end this shawl with 0.5 inches (1.25 cm) of plain weave and hem stitching. Tencel fringe is best twisted, as it tends to fray, so plan to take the time for this step! I like long fringe, so before twisting I cut the fringe to 8 inches (20.25 cm).

Have fun with the pattern! There are so many different color combinations you could use to create your own work of art!

Dimensions: 26 inches × 78 inches, plus 8-inch fringe
(66 × 198 cm, 20.25-cm fringe)

Warp
Sett: 20 epi, 10 dent reed, 2 threads per dent
Length: 3.5-yard (3.2-m) warp
Thread: 8/2 Tencel, Sapphire Combo: 520 ends plus 4 floating selvedges = 524 ends, 1,900 yards (1,737.4 m)

Weft
8/2 Tencel, Lemongrass: 1,250 yards (1,143 m)
Tabby: 8/2 Tencel, Sapphire Combo: 1,250 yards (1,143 m)

Threading
Alternate Motifs A and B: 9 times
Motif A: 1 time

Motif A
16 ends

B	B	B	B	B	B	B	B	B	B

Motif B
40 ends

Treadling
Work full pattern 20 times.
End with Motif A.
Add tabby after each pattern thread.

			T	T		
		4	4		4	
3	3				3	
	2		2	2		
1		1		1		
			X			Tabby
				X		
X						Motif A
	X					Repeat 16X
				X		Segue
					X	Repeat 3X
			X			Motif B
		X				Repeat 7X
				X		Segue
					X	Repeat 3X

52 | CARIBBEAN NIGHTS SHAWL

Scarves for Karen

Losing a friend is hard, no matter what the circumstances, and losing Karen was no exception. Her husband generously gave me her bamboo fiber, which she loved to weave with. In the mix were five different partial warps, all in Pearl. The number of ends varied from 18 to 46. All were over 5 yards. Hmmm, what to do? I knew I had enough warp for two scarves and a bit of bamboo left on the cone to use for the tabby, so I used this opportunity to show you a unique characteristic you can achieve with summer and winter. If you use only one threading block, you will create a double-sided woven piece. Just think of the possibilities! You could have stripes on one side and a solid on the other. Or simply a different color on each side!

For one scarf, I used a variegated Tencel against the Pearl. This scarf would be great to wear with blue jeans. The second scarf is all bamboo, but I wove the first half with blue and the second half with red. This approach put a total of three colors in the scarf. Both scarves have a wonderful drape, and, as they are narrow, they will be very comfortable to wear. And people will wonder how you did this magic.

Begin and end each scarf with 0.5 inches (1.25 cm) of plain weave and hem stitching. I completed the scarves with a twisted fringe, as the bamboo tends to separate and shed.

Just think of all the possibilities with this technique. While the Pearl warp might not be your favorite choice, I think Karen would be pleased.

Dimensions: 6 inches × 60 inches, plus 4-inch fringe (15.25 × 152.5 cm, 10.25-cm fringe)

Warp
Sett: 24 epi, 12 dent reed, 2 threads per dent
Thread: 10/2 bamboo, Pearl
- 1 scarf: 3-yard (2.7-m) warp; 144 ends plus 2 floating selvedges = 146 ends, 450 yards (411.5 m)
- 2 scarves: 5-yard (4.6-m) warp; 144 ends plus 2 floating selvedges = 146 ends, 750 yards (685.8 m)

Weft

Tencel/Bamboo Scarf
8/2 Tencel, Iris Combo: 300 yards (274.3 m)
Tabby: 10/2 bamboo, Pearl: 350 yards (320 m)

Multicolor Bamboo Scarf
10/2 bamboo
- Emperor Blue: 150 yards (137.2 m)
- China Red: 150 yards (137.2 m)

Tabby: 10/2 bamboo, Pearl: 350 yards (320 m)

Threading
Motif: 36 times

3		3	
	2		
			1

**Motif
4 ends**

Treadling
Repeat treadling to desired length.
Add tabby after each pattern thread.

	T		T	
3	3		3	
	2	2		
1		1		
		X		
			X		Tabby
X				
	X			

SCARVES FOR KAREN | 55

8-SHAFT PROJECTS

This chart is the key for substituting blocks into the threading drafts. Substitute all four threads for each lettered block in the charts. Some of the projects will use less than eight shafts but all of the treadles. Don't let that throw you. Just follow the charts.

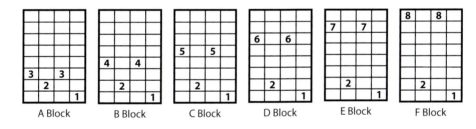

Key to blocks for 8-shaft projects

Blue Cubed Table Runner

This piece is a stash buster; I really don't like wasting fiber. I had several cones of various blues, none having more than 200 yards and most with less. Then I added that purple accent thread you see in this piece just to give a spark of color. In winding this warp, I was able to empty six cones. Of course, there is always a risk with this approach. You need to be sure to spread out the different colors to avoid a stripe. And there will always be that odd thread that stands out more than the others, which in this piece was the purple. Just let it be a part of the design.

You could make each motif a different color or make a one-color warp. Each motif uses 32 ends, so it would be an easy adjustment.

Since the warp was the darker colors, I used King Blue for the pattern thread. For the tabby thread, I used Deep Turquoise. These were the only two consistent colors in this piece. This point is indicated in the yardage requirements. Begin and end with 0.5 inches (1.25 cm) of plain weave and hem stitch. This is a lovely table runner for any home!

Dimensions: 17 inches × 40 inches, plus 3-inch fringe (43.25 × 101.5 in, 7.5-cm fringe)

Warp
Sett: 24 epi, 12 dent reed, 2 threads per dent
Length: 2.5-yard (2.3-m) warp
Threads: 10/2 perle cotton, multiple colors of blue: 416 ends plus 2 floating selvedges = 418 ends, 1,100 yards (1,005.8 m)

Weft
5/2 perle cotton, King Blue: 400 yards (365.8 m)
Tabby: 10/2 perle cotton, Deep Turquoise: 400 yards (365.8 m)

Threading
Alternate Motifs A and B: 6 times
Motif A: 1 time

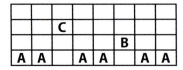

Motif A
32 ends

Motif B
32 ends

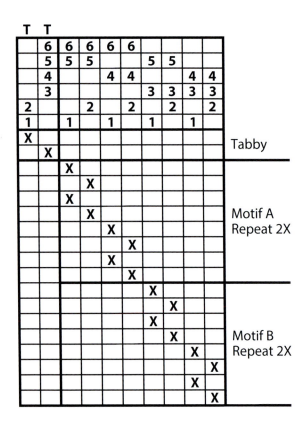

Tabby

Motif A
Repeat 2X

Motif B
Repeat 2X

Treadling
Alternate Motifs A and B to desired length.
End with Motif A.
Add tabby after each pattern thread.

60 | BLUE CUBED TABLE RUNNER

Bones Towels

This set of towels is perfect for the Halloween kitchen. It is also an easy pattern to change and make a one-of-a-kind table runner. You can increase the number of bones for a totally different look. Add a jack-o'-lantern and some candy corn to your table, and you are all set. Change the colors to make towels just to wipe your dogs' feet when they come in from outside. Or a rug on which to put your dog dishes! It is just a fun pattern to use in so many ways.

Begin with 2 inches (5 cm) of plain weave in Black 10/2 perle cotton, followed by 4 Orange, 2 White, and 4 Orange passes. This pattern follows the color threading sequence. Next, do 1 inch (2.5 cm) of Black, and finally one repeat of the motif. The plaid is then repeated 8 times or to your desired length. Finally, reverse the beginning sequence. Doing so will allow you to have a 1-inch (2.5-cm) rolled hem. There is enough warp to make two towels.

The treadling pattern is symmetrical, so you can treadle from top to bottom or vice versa.

Dimensions: 14 inches by 25 inches (35.5 × 63.5 cm)

Warp
Sett: 24 epi, 12 dent reed, 2 threads per dent
Length: 3-yard (2.7-m) warp
Threads: 10/2 perle cotton
- Black: 216 ends, 675 yards (617.2 m)
- White: 40 ends, 135 yards (123.4 m)
- Orange: 80 ends plus floating selvedges = 82 ends, 270 yards (246.9 m)

Weft
10/2 perle cotton
- Black (includes tabby): 600 yards (548.6 m)
- Orange: 75 yards (68.6 m)
- White: 40 yards (36.6 m)

Pattern thread: 5/2 perle cotton, white: 75 yards (68.6 m)

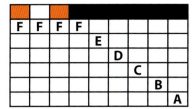

End Motif
36 ends

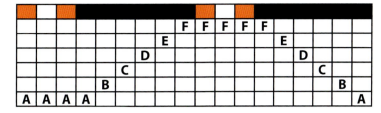

Full Motif
72 ends

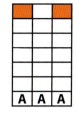

Beginning Motif
12 ends

> **Threading**
> Beginning Motif: 1 time
> Full Motif: 4 times
> End Motif: 1 time

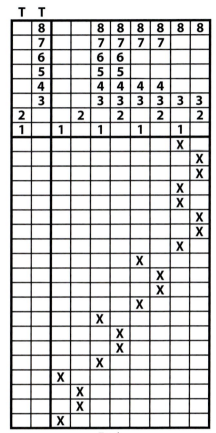

> **Treadling for Bone Motif**
> This motif is symmetrical, so you can treadle in either direction. Add tabby after each pattern thread.

BONES TOWELS | 63

BOO! Scarf

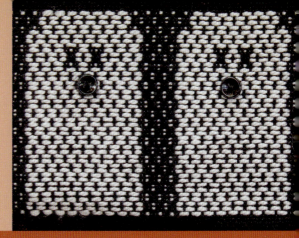

How fun is this scarf? You will definitely be noticed at Halloween when you wear this piece anywhere you go. It is ideal for a party or just to wear to the store. Unquestionably a head turner!

When weaving the ghosts, it is important to read the treadling from the bottom to the top; otherwise, the ghosts will be upside down. You could choose to do ghosts at both ends of the scarf for something different. In that case, in the second half you would read the treadling from the top down.

Begin the scarf with 1.5 inches (3.75 cm) of plain weave. Then weave 5 repeats of the ghosts. Now you will have woven a total of 17 inches (43.25 cm). Next, weave 20 inches (50.75 cm) of plain weave. At this point, you will begin to do the plain weave inlay of the "BOO!" Remember that the letters need to be upside down at this point. You are working on the down side of the scarf! Leave 0.5 inches (1.25 cm) between each letter. After the exclamation point, weave 2 inches (5 cm) of plain weave and then hem stitch. Refer to the inlay instructions on page 67.

You are done! Your scarf will be approximately 56 inches (142.25 cm). After wet finishing the scarf, I embellished the ghosts by giving them mouths, using tiny 6 mm black buttons. Have fun!

Dimensions: 6.5 inches × 56 inches, plus 4-inch fringe
(16.5 × 142.25 cm, 10.25-cm fringe)

Warp
Sett: 24 epi, 12 dent reed, 2 threads per dent
Length: 3-yard (2.7-m) warp
Thread: 10/2 perle cotton, Black: 156 ends plus 2 floating selvedges = 158 ends, 500 yards (457.2 m)

Weft
Pattern thread for ghosts and inlay: 5/2 perle cotton, White: 150 yards (137.2 m)
Tabby: 10/2 perle cotton, Black: 300 yards (274.3 m)

Threading
Full Motif: 3 times
Partial Motif: 1 time

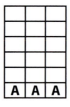

Partial Motif
12 ends

Full Motif
48 ends

Treadling for Ghost Motif
Treadle from the bottom up.
Add tabby after each pattern thread.

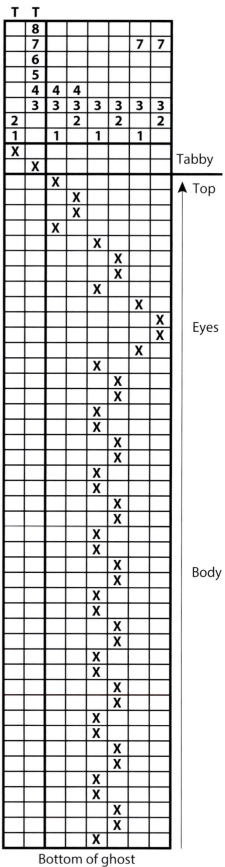

66 | BOO! SCARF

PLAIN WEAVE INLAY

Plain weave inlay is very easy to do. It can be used to add wonderful designs or words to a piece. In my description of this technique, I will be referencing the BOO! scarf.

Plan ahead! This is key to successful inlay. I made paper patterns to follow. The letters were upside down as I wove, and these patterns helped me to maintain the correct size and placement.

Since I had the patterns, I knew approximately how much of the warp I needed to save and where to begin the inlay.

Now to do the inlay! The thread used for the inlay is the same as the thread for the ghosts. The warp is 10/2; the inlay thread is 5/2. You could use any thread you like, but you should sample to make sure you are getting the look you want.

Each plain weave thread is followed by the inlay thread—in the same shed! I would place the plain weave thread, beat, place the inlay thread, beat. Then repeat back and forth. You will notice that I use small netting shuttles to hold the inlay thread. I find these very useful and especially great for this technique.

You can see my paper pattern lying beside the inlay. This was part of the exclamation point pattern. *Heddlecraft* magazine (January/February 2020) has a wonderful section on various types of inlay, each with its own advantage. If you haven't subscribed to this online magazine, I would encourage you to do so.

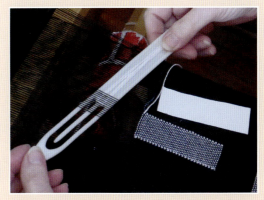

Picking up the warp threads for the inlay.

Inlay thread in place—now beat!

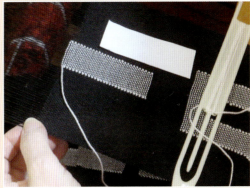

Inlay thread in place and beaten. Follow this with a plain weave thread.

◀ The paper patterns I used for BOO!

Christmas Lights Towels

These are wonderful sets of towels for the holiday season, and I've given you only two options for weaving them. It would be easy to add a plaid into the pattern or different colors of lights. I chose to go with the old-style lights that remind me of my childhood. Oh my, those lights got hot!

For the White-dominant towel, I wove 5 inches (12.75 cm) of plain weave and then 8 passes of Green, 4 passes of Red, 8 passes of Green, and then 12 passes of White. Then I began the motif. Do note that at the beginning you will treadle the motif from the bottom up so that your light bulb is hanging down. Then I repeated the colors as indicated above. Then I wove 6.5 inches (16.5 cm) of White plain weave. Now you are at the other end, where you will repeat the pattern motif, but this time you will treadle the motif from the top down so that once again your light is hanging correctly. Weave 4 passes of a high-contrast color and then weave the second towel.

For the 4-bulb colored towel, I followed the same procedure in the beginning. But after I treadled the first bulb, I put in only 5 passes of White plain weave. Then I began the second light. This took me to the center of the towel, where I wove 0.5 inches (1.25 cm) of White plain weave and then began the third and fourth set of lights. Always be aware of the direction of the light and treadle accordingly. Add a tabby thread between each pattern thread. Weave 4 passes of a high-contrast color, and then weave the second towel.

After the weaving was done and a 1-inch (2.5-cm) hem was finished, I embellished the lights with the never-ending, always tangled cord. Using a single strand of Wintergreen, I embroidered a simple running stitch. This step is optional.

CHRISTMAS LIGHTS TOWELS | 69

TWO-COLOR VERSION

Dimensions: 15.5 inches × 25 inches (39.25 × 63.5 cm)

Warp

Sett: 24 epi, 12 dent reed, 2 threads per dent

Length: 3-yard (2.7-m) warp

Threads: 10/2 perle cotton

- White: 332 ends, 1,000 yards (914.4 m)
- Sapphire: 32 ends plus 2 floating selvedges = 34 ends, 125 yards (114.3 m)
- Red: 8 ends, 40 yards (36.6 m)

Weft

10/2 perle cotton

- White (includes tabby): 600 yards (548.6 m)
- Red (stripe): 15 yards (13.7 m)
- Sapphire (stripe): 40 yards (36.6 m)

5/2 perle cotton

- Sapphire: 40 yards (36.6 m)
- Red: 40 yards (36.6 m)

Embroidered cord: 5/2 perle cotton, Wintergreen: 3 yards (2.7 m)

FOUR-COLOR VERSION

Dimensions: 15.5 inches × 25 inches (39.25 × 63.5 cm)

Warp

Sett: 24 epi, 12 dent reed, 2 threads per dent

Length: 3-yard (2.7-m) warp

Threads: 10/2 perle cotton

- White: 332 ends, 1,000 yards (914.4 m)
- Sapphire: 32 ends plus 2 floating selvedges = 34 ends, 125 yards (114.3 m)
- Red: 8 ends, 40 yards (36.6 m)

Weft

10/2 perle cotton

- White (includes tabby): 600 yards (548.6 m)
- Red (stripe): 15 yards (13.7 m)
- Sapphire (stripe): 40 yards (36.6 m)

5/2 perle cotton

- Sapphire: 20 yards (18.3 m)
- Red: 20 yards (18.3 m)
- Orange: 20 yards (18.3 m)
- Royal Blue: 20 yards (18.3 m)

Embroidered cord: 5/2 perle cotton, Wintergreen: 3 yards (2.7 m)

Threading
Border 1: 1 time
Alternate Motifs A
 and B: 4 times
Motif A: 1 time
Border 2: 1 time
Color is indicated
 for the Borders.

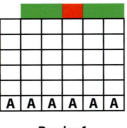

Border 1
24 ends

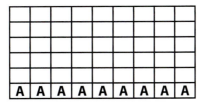

Motif A
36 ends

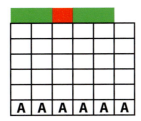

Motif B
36 ends

Border 2
24 ends

Treadling for Light Motif
Refer to text on page 69 for full description.
Add tabby after each pattern thread.

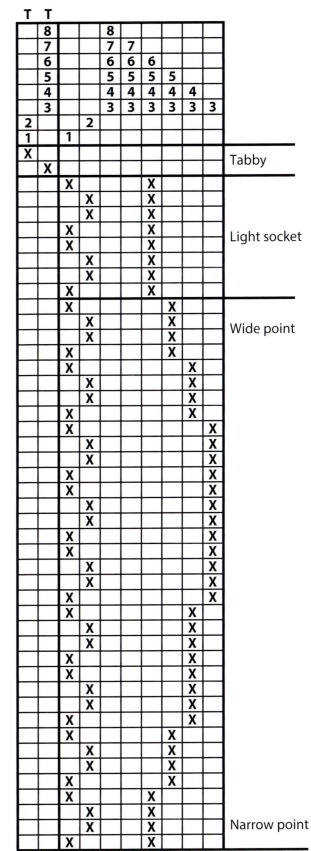

CHRISTMAS LIGHTS TOWELS | 71

Circle of Roses Scarf

Crabapple yarns makes some beautiful variegated perle cotton in 10/2, 5/2, and 3/2 sizes. This piece is an example of the colorway Concord. It has some purple specks, so instead of the rose color, a purple pattern thread would also have been a good choice. But I chose to split the difference and went with Lunatic Fringe 10 Red/Purple. One skein of the variegated fiber will be plenty for one scarf. You will have some left over to use another day. Now this scarf reminds me of a rose garden. It makes a wonderful scarf, but you could increase the width and have a lovely table runner.

Begin and end this piece with plain weave, hem stitching, and fringe.

Dimensions: 7.5 inches × 64 inches, plus 3-inch fringe
(19 × 162.5 cm, 7.5-cm fringe)

Warp
Sett: 24 epi, 12 dent reed, 2 threads per dent
Length: 3-yard (2.7-m) warp
Thread: 10/2 perle cotton, Concord by Crabapple Yarns: 188 ends plus 2 floating selvedges = 190 ends, 600 yards (548.6 m)

Weft
5/2 perle cotton, 10 Red/Purple by Lunatic Fringe: 300 yards (274.3 m)
Tabby: 10/2 perle cotton, Concord by Crabapple Yarns: 300 yards (274.3 m)

Border 2
16 ends

Motif B
12 ends

Motif A
44 ends

Border 1
16 ends

Threading
Border 1: 1 time
Alternate Motifs A and B: 2 times
Motif A: 1 time
Border 2: 1 time

Treadling
Alternate Motifs A and B to desired length. Add tabby after each pattern thread.

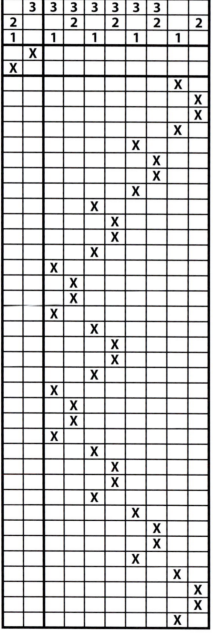

Motif B

Motif A

74 | CIRCLE OF ROSES SCARF

Coffee and Cream Scarf

The tiny diamonds created by the weave structure give the scarf the look of petit point needlework. The colors remind me of a hot cup of coffee with cream. I take mine with a splash of vanilla caramel flavoring. How about you? This is a perfect scarf for the fall wardrobe, especially if you have a camel-colored jacket. The contrast of the light and dark gives the diamonds dimension, with the lighter color receding and the dark brown moving forward. You could change the color combination to fit your wardrobe.

Begin and end this piece with 0.5 inches (1.25 cm) of plain weave and then hem stitch each end. I left a 4-inch (10.25 cm) fringe for my scarf. If you prefer, you can weave 1.5 inches (3.75 cm) of plain weave and finish with a rolled hem.

Dimensions: 7 inches × 62 inches, plus 4-inch fringe
(17.75 × 157.5 cm, 10.25-cm fringe)

Warp
Sett: 24 epi, 12 dent reed, 2 threads per dent
Length: 3-yard (2.7-m) warp
Thread: 10/2 perle cotton, Oak: 172 ends plus 2 floating selvedges = 174 ends, 550 yards (502.9 m)

Weft
5/2 perle cotton, Brown: 300 yards (274.3 m)
Tabby: 10/2 perle cotton, Oak: 300 yards (274.3 m)

Color Play Placemat

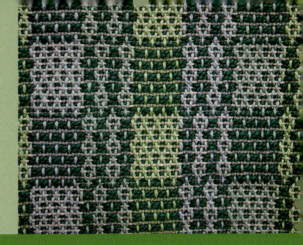

These placemats are named as such because we are now *playing* with color! This is such a great way to see the interaction of color in small threads. We used only four thread colors, but if you stand back and look at your placemats, you will also see mustard yellow, salmon, and orange, to name just a few new colors! But you don't have to use the colors I've given you. Feel free to substitute colors you like. Or you could use just one color. This set of four placemats and four napkins would make a great wedding gift.

The 5/2 Sapphire Green is used for the pattern thread in the weft. Each motif has a different color tabby thread. I followed the color pattern in the threading for the tabby threads. Because you change the tabby after each motif, you have a clear-cut place to change colors.

I began and ended each placemat and napkin with hem stitching. The fringe is 0.5 inches (1.25 cm). You could also do a rolled hem either by hand or using a serger.

Dimensions: Placemat: 13 inches × 16 inches (33 × 40.75 cm); Napkin: 13 inches × 13 inches (33 × 33 cm)

Warp
Sett: 24 epi, 12 dent reed, 2 threads per dent
Length: 5-yard (4.6-m) warp
Threads: 10/2 perle cotton
- Mint: 96 ends plus 2 floating selvedges = 98 ends, 500 yards (457.2 m)
- Light Yellow: 72 ends, 375 yards (342.9 m)
- Poplin: 72 ends, 375 yards (342.9 m)
- Tea: 72 ends, 375 yards (342.9 m)

Weft
5/2 perle cotton, Sapphire: 600 yards (548.6 m)
10/2 perle cotton
- Mint: 200 yards (182.9 m)
- Light Yellow: 200 yards (182.9 m)
- Poplin: 200 yards (182.9 m)
- Tea: 200 yards (182.9 m)

Includes yardage for the tabby and 4 napkins.

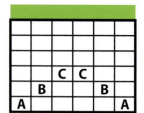

Partial Motif
24 ends

Full Motif
96 ends

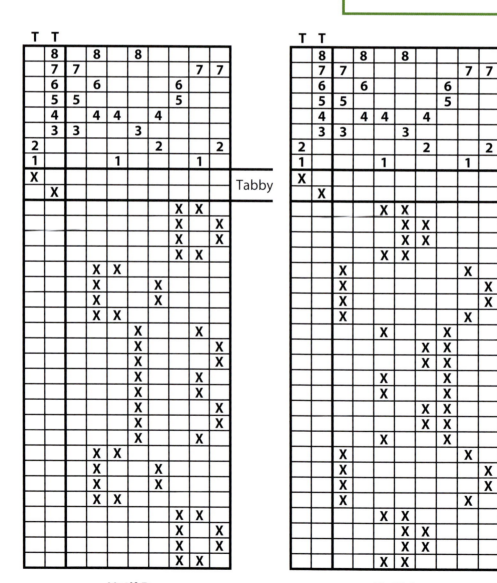

Threading
Full Motif: 3 times
Partial Motif: 1 time
Follow color code at top of threading chart.

Treadling
Alternate Motifs A and B: 8 times
Motif A: 1 time
Add tabby after each pattern thread.
Refer to description on page 79 for more information.

Motif B

Motif A

80 | COLOR PLAY PLACEMAT

Easter Eggs One and Two Table Runners

Adapted from a draft by Robyn Spady

This is the perfect runner for the Easter season! Since there are so many color changes, it is a great way to use up those partial cones of thread. If you don't have a variety of 5/2 cotton spools, remember that you can use two threads of 10/2 together, and voila! . . . you have 5/2 thread! I used four colors in my eggs, beginning and ending with the same color but alternating the placement. You can choose any colors—and as many as you want—for your eggs.

For Easter Eggs One, the sequencing of the Green weft is the same as in the warp—20 threads and then White—so begin and end the piece with 20 passes of Green and hem stitching. Then put 20 threads of Green in between each egg. You could also leave this out entirely in both the warp and the weft.

When I treadled the eggs, I began and ended each block with four passes of White thread before I began the egg design. Doing so framed the egg nicely. You can change this approach to suit your preferences.

For Easter Eggs Two, I followed the sequence of the colors in the warp: 8 Green, 4 White, 8 Green, and then the pattern block. Instead of Easter eggs over the whole piece, I chose to put only two rows of eggs at each end. Then I repeated the plaid in the center.

Note: The egg pattern is not symmetrical vertically, so you need to plan ahead. When reading the treadling sequence, treadle one egg from the top down. The next egg is treadled from the bottom up. This approach changes the direction of the eggs so that they aren't all facing one direction. You could change this arrangement and put half of the eggs facing one direction. Then, at the halfway point, change the direction of the treadling so that the eggs are facing the opposite direction.

EASTER EGGS ONE VERSION

Dimensions: 16.5 inches × 32 inches, plus 4-inch fringe
(42 × 81.25 cm, 10.25-cm fringe)

Warp

Sett: 24 epi, 12 dent reed, 2 threads per dent
Length: 2.5-yard (2.3-m) warp
Threads: 10/2 perle cotton

- Scarab: 140 ends plus 2 floating selvedges = 142 ends, 375 yards (342.9 m)
- White: 264 ends, 700 yards (640.1 m)

Weft

Tabby: 10/2 perle cotton

- White (includes tabby): 350 yards (320 m)
- Green: 100 yards (91.4 m)

5/2 perle cotton

- Deep Turquoise: 125 yards (114.3 m)
- Bali: 125 yards (114.3 m)
- Purple: 125 yards (114.3 m)
- Coral by Lunatic Fringe: 125 yards (114.3 m)

EASTER EGGS TWO VERSION

Dimensions: 15 inches × 48 inches, plus 3-inch fringe
(38 × 122 cm, 7.5-cm fringe)

Warp

Sett: 24 epi, 12 dent reed, 2 threads per dent
Length: 3-yard (2.7-m) warp
Threads: 10/2 perle cotton

- White: 252 ends, 800 yards (731.5 m)
- Scarab: 112 ends plus 2 floating selvedges = 114 ends, 375 yards (342.9 m)

Weft

Tabby: 10/2 perle cotton

- White: 350 yards (320 m)
- Scarab: 250 yards (228.6 m)

5/2 perle cotton, all colors by Lunatic Fringe

- Coral: 12 yards (11 m)
- Sky Blue: 12 yards (11 m)
- 10 Green Yellow: 12 yards (11 m)
- 10 Purple: 12 yards (11 m)

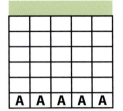

Partial Motif
20 ends

Full Motif
64 ends

Threading for Easter Eggs One
Full Motif: 6 times
Partial Motif: 1 time
Colors are indicated above threading chart.

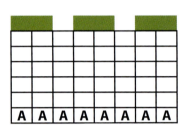

Border 2
32 ends

Border 1
12 ends

Full Motif
64 ends

Threading for Easter Egg Two
Border 1: 1 time
Full Motif: 5 times
Border 2: 1 time
Colors are indicated above threading chart.

Treadling for Easter Eggs One and Two
Read instructions on page 81 for treadling.
Add tabby between each pattern thread.

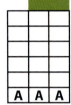

84 | EASTER EGGS ONE AND TWO TABLE RUNNERS

Birthday Celebration Table Runner

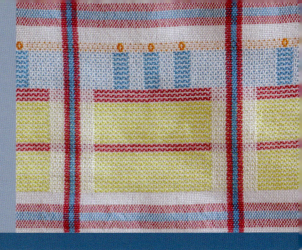

This is the perfect runner for that big birthday bash! Change the color/flavor of the cake to chocolate, spice, or even red velvet. You can also change the color/flavor of the icing. (My personal preference is chocolate cake with peanut butter frosting!) There are no limits to color combinations. You can also make your cake multi-layered with different-colored cakes or icings.

How about weaving this runner for a child or grandchild's first birthday? Then embroider the names and birth dates of the parents along with the child onto the runner. As more family members are added, embroider their names and birth dates as well. This is sure to become a keepsake for the recipient.

Weave 3 inches (7.5 cm) of White plain weave, followed by 4 passes of Coral, 4 passes of Sky Blue, and 4 passes of Coral. Next, weave 8 plain weave passes in White. Now you are ready to begin the cake motif. Since this is a directional motif, you will need to read the treadling from the bottom up for the first cake. After you have woven the cake motif, weave another 8 passes of White plain weave followed by the Coral/Sky Blue stripe combination. Next, weave 4.5 inches (11.5 cm) of White plain weave followed by the stripes. Repeat these steps 4 times. Now you are ready to weave the second cake motif. This time you will read the treadling pattern from the top down. Weave another 8 passes of White plain weave, followed by the Coral/Sky Blue stripe, and finish with 3 inches (7.5 cm) of White plain weave. I finished the runner with a rolled hem, but you could also have fringe if you prefer.

Dimensions: 16.5 inches × 38 inches (42 × 96.5 cm)

Warp
Sett: 24 epi, 12 dent reed, 2 threads per dent
Length: 2.25-yard (2.1-m) warp
Threads: 10/2 perle cotton
- White: 348 ends, 800 yards (731.5 m)

5/2 perle cotton, all colors by Lunatic Fringe
- Coral: 32 ends plus 2 floating selvedges = 34 ends, 90 yards (82.3 m)
- Sky Blue: 16 ends, 45 yards (41.2 m)

Weft
Tabby: 10/2 perle cotton, White: 550 yards (502.9 m)

5/2 perle cotton, all colors by Lunatic Fringe
- Butter (cake): 25 yards (22.9 m)
- Coral (icing): 50 yards (45.7 m)
- Sky Blue (candles): 40 yards (36.6 m)
- 10 Yellow Red (candle flame): 4 yards (3.7 m)

Threading
Alternate Motifs A and B: 3 times
Motif A: 1 time

Motif A
12 ends

Motif B
116 ends

Treadling
Treadle from the bottom up for the first cake; for the second cake, treadle from the top down.
Add tabby after each pattern thread.

- Tabby
- 1X Candle flame
- 8X Candles
- 3X Icing
- 9X Top cake layer
- 2X Center icing
- 9X Bottom cake layer

BIRTHDAY CELEBRATION TABLE RUNNER | 87

Eire Spring Table Runner

This is the perfect piece to use up some of those cones with small amounts of thread. I was able to empty four cones for this project. Choose colors that you like, whether you use one color or six colors. As designed, this runner is narrow and perfect for a side table, but the draft is very simple and the width can be easily increased or decreased. This draft would make a lovely scarf!

I had more of the Bali color than the other three colors, so I let the Bali be more dominant in the warp. I began with Bali and then alternated Bali and one of the other colors, finally ending with Bali. The borders are also in Bali.

For the tabby, I had enough of all four greens to just alternate one green per motif. It seems a bit tedious changing the tabby so often, but the final result is stunning.

Look at your shelf to see whether you have some cones that might be just the thing for your own runner. Using different colors can be fun as you watch the interaction of the threads and see new colors emerging. Have fun with this pattern!

Dimensions: 12 inches × 46 inches, plus 3-inch fringe (30.5 × 116.75 cm, 7.5-cm fringe)

Warp
Sett: 24 epi, 12 dent reed, 2 threads per dent
Length: 2.5-yard (2.3 m) warp
Threads: 10/2 perle cotton
- Bali: 172 ends plus 2 floating selvedges = 174 ends, 450 yards (411.5 m)
- 10 Green by Lunatic Fringe: 40 ends, 125 yards (114.3 m)
- 5 Green by Lunatic Fringe: 40 ends, 125 yards (114.3 m)
- 5 Green Yellow by Lunatic Fringe: 40 ends, 125 yards (114.3 m)

Weft
5/2 perle cotton, White: 425 yards (388.6 m)
Tabby: 10/2 perle cotton
- Bali: 125 yards (114.3 m)
- 10 Green by Lunatic Fringe: 125 yards (114.3 m)
- 5 Green by Lunatic Fringe: 125 yards (114.3 m)
- 5 Green Yellow by Lunatic Fringe: 125 yards (114.3 m)

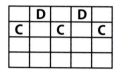
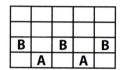

Border 2
16 ends

Motif B
20 ends

Motif A
20 ends

Border 1
16 ends

Threading
Border 1: 1 time
Alternate Motifs A and B: 6 times
Motif A: 1 time
Border 2: 1 time

Treadling
Alternate Motifs A and B to desired length.
End with Motif A.
Add tabby after each pattern thread.

90 | EIRE SPRING TABLE RUNNER

Lace Runner

This runner reminds me of lace with all of the circles within circles. It also has similarities to overshot. It is simply a beautiful piece. I dressed the loom with a dark blue warp, which I had planned to use for the tabby in the weft. But when I started to weave, it just seemed a bit drab and flat. So instead of using the blue thread for the tabby, I decided to go with purple. What a difference that made! Now the runner takes on an iridescent quality in the light, giving the runner much more visual appeal. Don't hesitate to mix colors to see what happens. Just be careful of colors opposite on the color wheel, as they tend to get muddy. I repeated Motifs A and B six times and ended with Motif A for balance. There are 0.5 inches (1.25 cm) of plain weave at the beginning and end, and 3 inches (7.5 cm) of fringe finish the piece. You could also do a rolled hem by weaving 1.5 inches (3.75 cm) of plain weave.

> **Dimensions:** 15 inches × 42 inches, plus 3-inch fringe
> (38 × 106.75 cm, 7.5-cm fringe)
>
> **Warp**
> **Sett:** 24 epi, 12 dent reed, 2 threads per dent
> **Length:** 2.5-yard (2.3-m) warp
> **Thread:** 10/2 perle cotton, Soldier Blue: 364 ends plus 2 floating selvedges = 366 ends, 1,000 yards (914.4 m)
>
> **Weft**
> 5/2 perle cotton, White: 450 yards (411.5 m)
> **Tabby:** 10/2 perle cotton, Purple: 475 yards (434.3 m)

D						D
	C				C	
		B		B		
			A			

Motif A
28 ends

							D		D		D		D							
				C		C		C		C		C		C		C				
	B		B		B										B		B		B	
A		A																A		A

Motif B
84 ends

Threading
Alternate Motifs A and B: 3 times
Motif A: 1 time

T	T									
	6	6	6					6	6	
	5	5	5	5	5					
	4			4	4	4	4			
	3					3	3	3	3	
2			2		2		2		2	
1		1		1		1		1		
X										Tabby
	X									
								X		Begin
									X	
									X	
								X		
						X				
							X			
							X			
						X				
				X						
					X					
					X					
				X						
		X								
			X							
			X							
		X								
				X						
					X					
					X					
				X						
						X				
							X			
							X			
						X				
								X		
									X	
									X	
								X		End

Motif A

Treadling
Alternate Motifs A and B to desired length.
End with Motif A.
Add tabby after each pattern thread.

treadling continued on next page

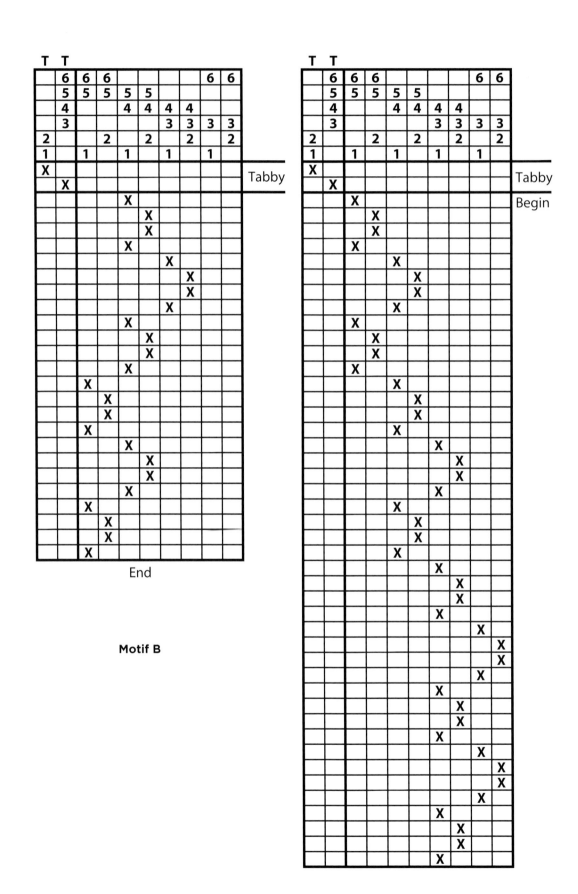

Motif B

94 | LACE RUNNER

Peaks and Valleys Scarf

One look at this scarf and I imagine you thought it was a broken twill. In a sense, it is, but instead of weaving it as twill, it is now woven as summer and winter. Having the summer and winter shapes creates a whole new look. And the summer and winter diamond motifs really stand out.

This scarf would be lovely in any color, but I chose two completely different colors to get an iridescent look. Another combination could be a red warp and yellow tabby for a striking sunset effect. Try using a variegated 10/2 perle cotton and a high-contrast pattern thread for another unique look. It would be easy to make a wider scarf simply by adding another motif. This piece would be a great scarf for a first summer and winter project, as it is a very simple pattern. Begin and end with 0.5 inches (1.25 cm) of plain weave and hem stitching.

Dimensions: 6 inches × 64 inches, plus 4-inch fringe (15.25 × 162.5 cm)

Warp
Sett: 24 epi, 12 dent reed, 2 threads per dent
Length: 3-yard (2.7-m) warp
Thread: 10/2 perle cotton, Bali: 144 ends plus 2 floating selvedges = 146 ends, 450 yards (411.5 m)

Weft
5/2 perle cotton, Wintergreen: 275 yards (251.5 m)
Tabby: 10/2 perle cotton, Yellow: 275 yards (251.5 m)

Threading
Motif: 3 times

	D				D			D		
C				C				C		
		B			B				B	
			A				A			A

Motif
48 ends

Treadling

Repeat treadling motif to desired length. Add tabby after each pattern thread.

T	T								
	6	6	6					6	6
	5	5	5	5	5				
	4			4	4	4	4		
	3				3	3	3	3	
2			2		2		2		2
1		1		1		1		1	
X									
	X									← Tabby
			X						
		X							
		X							
			X						
				X					
				X					
				X					
					X				
						X			
					X				
					X				
						X			
							X		
							X		
							X		
								X	

Peonies Scarf

Peonies are such beautiful spring flowers. They have that dark green foliage with those lush, spectacular flowers. I just wish they lasted longer! Fortunately, the foliage lasts all summer even if the flowers are temporary. This scarf reminds me of those gorgeous leaf colors. Give this scarf a twist when you wear it, allowing both sides to show. It will definitely make an impression.

I used Lang Linello for my pattern thread; there are many color options to choose from in this yarn. The long color repeat is perfect for weaving this scarf. When winding your bobbins, remember to wind the bobbin and then wind *that* bobbin a second time so that you are matching the color ends properly. You will have to do this will *all* bobbins, first to last. Begin and end with 0.5 inches (1.25 cm) of plain weave and hem stitching. I left a 4-inch (10.25-cm) fringe, but you could increase or decrease to suit yourself. Have fun weaving this scarf!

Dimensions: 7 inches × 64 inches, plus 4-inch fringe
(17.75 × 162.5 cm, 10.25-cm fringe)

Warp
Sett: 24 epi, 12 dent reed, 2 threads per dent
Length: 3-yard (2.7-m) warp
Thread: 10/2 perle cotton, Evergreen: 172 ends plus 2 floating selvedges = 174 ends, 550 yards (502.9 m)

Weft
Lang Linello Pastel, 1 skein = 360 yards (280 m). *You will use approximately 275 yards (251.5 m).*
Tabby: 10/2 perle cotton, Evergreen: 300 yards (274.3 m)

Threading
Full Motif: 3 times
Partial Motif: 1 time

Partial Motif
4 ends

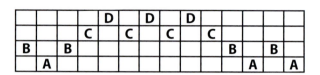

Full Motif
56 ends

Treadling
Alternate Motifs A and B to desired length. End with Motif A. Add tabby after each pattern thread.

Motif B

Motif A

100 | PEONIES SCARF

Pinwheels Scarf

This design is a very simple geometric, but it is really highlighted with the use of the Chroma fingering weight variegated yarn. The color repeat for this yarn is quite long and moves smoothly from one color to another, which is why it is successful. Self-striping sock yarns—yarns with a short repeat or abrupt color change—generally do not work well. KnitPicks has other color combinations that you could use. You should also notice that you have enough fingering weight yarn for two scarves, so plan accordingly. You might want to get an early start on Christmas or birthday presents!

This would be a fun scarf or table runner to make for a Fourth of July celebration. You would alternate weaving the motifs with red or blue fingering yarn and use a white warp and tabby. Begin and end with 0.5 inches (1.25 cm) of plain weave and hem stitching.

Dimensions: 7.5 inches × 62 inches, plus a 4-inch fringe
(19 × 157.5 cm, 10.25-cm fringe)

Warp
Sett: 24 epi, 12 dent reed, 2 ends
  per inch
Length: 3-yard (2.7-m) warp
Thread: 10/2 perle cotton, Bali:
  160 ends plus 2 floating selvedges =
  162 ends, 500 yards (457.2 m)

Weft
Chroma Fingering Weight Pegasus
  by KnitPicks: 396 yards (362.1 m) =
  1 skein. *You will use approximately*
  250 yards (228.6 m).
Tabby: 10/2 perle cotton, Bali:
  300 yards (274.3 m)

Full Motif
80 ends

Threading
Full Motif: 2 times

Treadling
Full Motif: 23 times or to desired length. Add tabby after each pattern thread.

D	D	D	D	D							
					C	C	C	C	C		
								B	B	B	B	B
											A	A	A	A	A

Full Motif

T T

	6			6	6				
	5			5	5	5	5	5	5
	4	4	4	4	4	4	4		
	3				3	3			
2			2		2		2		2
1		1		1		1		1	

| X | | | | | | | | | | Tabby |
| | X | | | | | | | | | |

		X								Repeat 3X
	X									
	X									
		X								

			X							Repeat 3X
		X								
		X								
			X							

				X						Repeat 3X
			X							
			X							
				X						

					X					Repeat 3X
				X						
				X						
					X					

Scarf Set

Two scarves, same pattern—but oh, so different! The lavender scarf uses two different shades of lavender and purple, but the dark purple pattern thread is the same size as the warp: 10/2. This creates a much softer image.

The green scarf uses Cranberry brand variegated cotton for the warp. This variegated thread has a dark green accent, which I matched for the pattern thread. In this scarf, the green pattern thread is twice the size of the warp thread: 5/2. For the tabby thread, I used the color Tea, as it matches perfectly with the Cranberry variegated thread.

Notice that there is a partial threading to balance the piece. In many of the summer and winter patterns, this approach really isn't necessary; however, these scarves require this short threading to complete the motif.

You have a choice! Pick which threading and thread size you like the best. It's always nice to have options.

Begin and end with 0.5 inches (1.25 cm) of plain weave and hem stitching.

LAVENDER VERSION
Dimensions: 7.5 inches × 64 inches, plus 4-inch fringe (19 × 162.5 cm, 10.25-cm fringe)

Warp
Sett: 24 epi, 12 dent reed, 2 threads per dent
Length: 3-yard (2.7-m) warp
Thread: 10/2 perle cotton, Grotto: 185 ends plus 2 floating selvedges = 187 ends, 600 yards (548.6 m)

Weft
10/2 perle cotton, Purple: 350 yards (320 m)
Tabby: 10/2 perle cotton, Grotto: 350 yards (320 m)

GREEN VERSION
Dimensions: 7.5 inches × 64 inches, plus 4-inch fringe (19 × 162.5 cm, 10.25-cm fringe)

Warp
Sett: 24 epi, 12 dent reed, 2 threads per dent
Length: 3-yard (2.7-m) warp
Thread: 10/2 perle cotton, Peonies by Crabapple: 189 ends plus 2 floating selvedges = 191 ends, 600 yards (548.6 m)

Weft
5/2 perle cotton, Evergreen: 300 yards (274.3 m)
Tabby: 10/2 perle cotton, Tea: 325 yards (297.2 m)

Threading for Lavender Version
Motifs A, B, B in sequence: 2 times
Motif A: 1 time
Partial Motif: 1 time

Threading for Green Version
Motifs A and B: 3 times
Motif A: 1 time
Partial Motif: 1 time

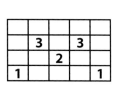

Partial Motif
5 ends

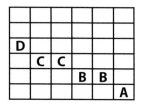

Motif B
24 ends

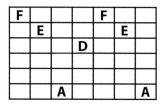

Motif A
28 ends

Treadling
Repeat complete treadling to desired length.
Add tabby after each pattern thread.

106 | SCARF SET

Seasons Table Runner

Adapted from a draft by Robyn Spady

This was such a fun piece to design and weave. You could easily change this runner to fit your requirements. Maybe you don't have as many colors on your shelf as I do, so you might make a smaller runner or repeat a color. Don't forget that you can use two strands of 10/2 perle cotton in lieu of one strand of 5/2 perle cotton. It's a bit more tedious to work with, but you ultimately get the same result.

To help you plan, each tree finished at 2.5 inches (6.25 cm), not including the 0.5 inches (1.25 cm) before and after each tree. Use this knowledge to calculate how many trees you need to get the length you want. Regarding the 0.5 inches (1.25 cm) of plain weave between each row of trees, you can increase, decrease, or leave this part out completely. The central motif consists of 0.5 inches (1.25 cm) of plain weave, followed by *one* repeat of the treadling for the trunk, and then finishing with 0.5 inches (1.25 cm) of plain weave. Again, this part can be increased, decreased, or left out completely for your runner. Begin and end this piece with 0.5 inches (1.25 cm) of plain weave and hem stitch.

Do you have a wedding coming up in the fall? This pattern would also make a beautiful set of towels for a gift. Change up the colors and make Christmas trees. You could embellish these with beads, sequins, or embroidery. Have fun!

Dimensions: 15.5 inches × 46 inches, plus 2-inch fringe (39.25 × 116.75 cm, 5-cm fringe)

Warp
Sett: 24 epi, 12 dent reed, 2 threads per dent
Length: 2.5-yard (2.3-m) warp
Thread: 10/2 perle cotton, Flaxon: 380 ends plus 2 floating selvedges = 382 ends, 1,000 yards (914.4 m)

Weft
5/2 perle cotton
- White: 30 yards (27.4 m)
- Scarab: 30 yards (27.4 m)
- Sapphire: 30 yards (27.4 m)
- Evergreen: 30 yards (27.4 m)
- Avocado: 30 yards (27.4 m)
- Gold: 30 yards (27.4 m)
- Rust: 30 yards (27.4 m)
- Burnt Orange: 30 yards (27.4 m)
- Brown: 75 yards (68.6 m)

Tabby: 10/2 perle cotton, Flaxon: 375 yards (342.9 m)

Threading

Motif: 7 times

Partial Motif: 1 time

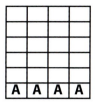

Partial Motif
16 ends

Motif
52 ends

Treadling

Refer to the text on page 107 for complete instructions. Add tabby after each pattern thread.

Tabby

Tree trunk
Repeat 2X

Bottom of tree

Top of tree

SEASONS TABLE RUNNER | 109

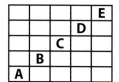

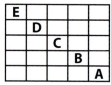

Border 2
20 ends

Partial Motif
4 ends

Full Motif
32 ends

Border 1
20 ends

Threading
Border 1: 1 time
Full Motif: 5 times
Partial Motif: 1 time
Border 2: 1 time

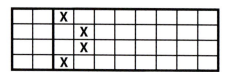

Partial Motif

Treadling
Full Motif: 41 times or to desired length
End with Partial Motif.
Add tabby after each pattern thread.

Full Motif

112 | SHADES OF GREEN SCARF

Sunspots Table Runner

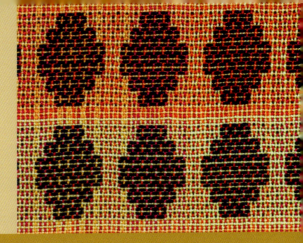

This is a very colorful and vibrant piece, sure to make a statement on any table. The warp is made up of a variety of colors. I wanted to use up those little bits on cones, so I pulled colors from the same family and warped the loom randomly so that no stripes would be evident. I was able to empty eight cones! When it came to the tabby thread, I chose two colors and alternated them. As I wanted the spots to be separated, I wove six passes of tabby between each spot—three Orange and three Yellow. But you could choose any color you like for the tabby and arrange it to suit you.

Begin and end the piece with 0.5 inches (1.25 cm) of plain weave and hem stitching, or, if you prefer, weave 1.5 inches (3.75 cm) of plain weave and do a rolled hem.

Dimensions: 15.5 inches × 42 inches, plus 3-inch fringe
(39.25 × 106.75 cm, 7.5-cm fringe)

Warp
Sett: 24 epi, 12 dent reed, 2 threads per dent
Length: 2.5-yard (2.3-m) warp
Threads: 10/2 perle cotton, variety of colors (I used bright reds, oranges, and yellows): 376 ends plus 2 floating selvedges = 378 ends, 1,000 yards (914.4 m)

Weft
5/2 perle cotton, Black: 350 yards (228.6 m)
Tabby: 10/2 perle cotton
- Yellow: 175 yards (160 m)
- Orange: 175 yards (160 m)

Border
4 ends

Threading
Border: 1 time
Full Motif: 10 times
Partial Motif: 1 time
Border: 1 time

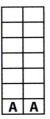

Full Motif
36 ends

Partial Motif
8 ends

Treadling
Motif: 23 times or to desired length
Add tabby after each pattern thread.

SUNSPOTS TABLE RUNNER | 115

Woodland Runner

The Woodland Runner is an incredibly easy but spectacular runner that will really impress your guests! Since this piece is woven in summer and winter fashion, both sides are equally attractive. If you want to make gifts in many different colors, put on a White warp and just change the color of the pattern thread for each. To make matching placemats, eliminate a tree on one side and extend the central motif.

Begin and end this runner with 0.5 inches (1.25 cm) of plain weave and hem stitch. I left a 3-inch (7.5-cm) fringe, but you could also weave 1.5 inches (3.75 cm) of plain weave and finish with a rolled hem.

Dimensions: 13 inches × 36 inches, plus 3-inch fringe
(33 × 91.5 cm, 7.5-cm fringe)

Warp
Sett: 24 epi, 12 dent reed, 2 threads per dent
Length: 2.5-yard (2.3-m) warp
Thread: 10/2 perle cotton, Wintergreen: 316 ends plus 2 floating selvedges = 318 ends, 835 yards (763.5 m)

Weft
5/2 perle cotton, White: 350 yards (320 m)
Tabby: 10/2 perle cotton, Wintergreen: 350 yards (320 m)

> **Threading**
> Full Motif: 1 time
> 316 ends

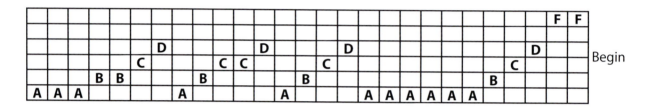

Treadling

Repeat treadling until you have 8 trees or to desired length.
Repeat each block as indicated in the draft.
Add tabby after each pattern thread.

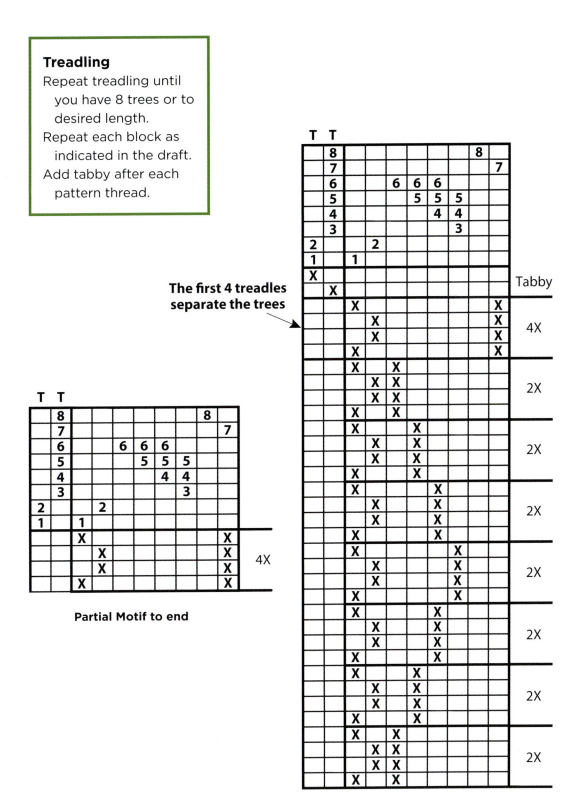

Partial Motif to end

Full Motif

WOODLAND RUNNER | 119

Smitten with Kittens Table Runner

I am a total pushover for any cat or kitten. It probably has to do with being raised on a dairy farm where cats were everywhere. No mice . . . just cats! This table runner showcases my fondness, with multiple cats just running amok.

I chose to use a variegated thread for the warp to give some pizzazz to the piece. But to prevent it from becoming too dark, I used White for the tabby. There were many colors in the warp to choose from, but I settled on Moss Green, as my cats are playing in the yard. I chose Black for the cats so they would really stand out.

Begin with 0.5 inches (1.25 cm) of plain weave in White and hem stitching. Then weave four passes of the Moss Green. Next are six passes of White, and then weave the cat motif. Follow this section with six more passes of White and then repeat the process. Remember, this motif is directional! The first seven cats you need to weave from the tail up. At the midpoint, you will weave the remaining seven cats from the top down. The treadling pattern indicates the position of the cat. Finish your runner with 0.5 inches (1.25 cm) of plain weave and hem stitching. I chose to leave 3 inches (7.5 cm) of fringe, although you could weave additional plain weave and finish with a rolled hem.

When planning your own runner, use colors that suit your decor. Try a darker color palette for the background and then have lighter-colored cats. And, of course, you can weave any number of cats. You might choose to just put cats on the ends as a border. How about adjusting the draft to weave scarves or even valances? So many ideas! I hope you enjoy this pattern as much as I loved creating it.

Dimensions: 15.5 inches × 42 inches, plus 3-inch fringe (39.25 × 106.75 cm, 7.5-cm fringe)

Warp
Sett: 24 epi, 12 dent reed, 2 threads per dent
Length: 2.5-yard (2.3-m) warp
Threads: 10/2 perle cotton, Smitten by Crabapple Yarns: 324 ends, 850 yards (777.2 m)
5/2 perle cotton, Moss Green: 56 ends plus 2 floating selvedges = 58 ends, 150 yards (137.2 m)

Weft
Tabby: 10/2 perle cotton, White: 550 yards (502.9 m)
5/2 perle cotton
- Moss Green, 45 yards (41.2 m)
- Black, 200 yards (182.9 m)

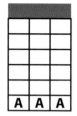

Border
12 ends

> **Threading**
> Border: 1 time
> Alternate Motifs A and B: 8 times
> Motif A: 1 time
> Border: 1 time

Motif A
36 ends

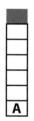

Motif B
4 ends

> **Treadling**
> 1 full repeat is 1 cat.
> Add tabby after each pattern thread.

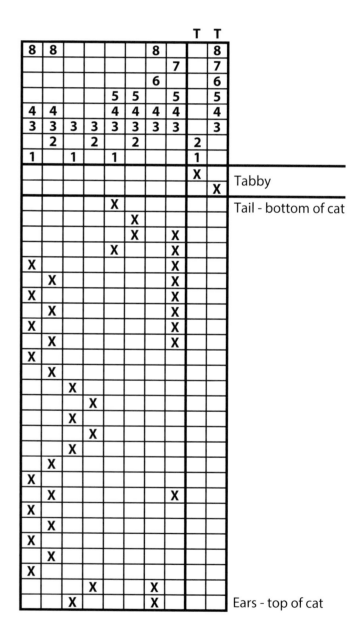

122 | SMITTEN WITH KITTENS TABLE RUNNER

Hanukkah Runner

This is a special runner for a special holiday! It is simple and yet elegant. The large span of white gives you plenty of room for your cookies and other special treats.

Begin this runner with 0.5 inches (1.25 cm) of plain weave and hem stitching. Next, follow this pattern: 8 passes Blue, 6 passes White, 4 passes Blue, 4 passes White, 2 passes Blue, ending with 12 passes of White. Then you will begin the candle motif. Do note that the candles are directional, so you need to be sure your candles are standing in the correct direction. Be sure to add a tabby after each pattern thread.

After you have woven your candle motif, you will weave 26 inches (66 cm) of White plain weave. Next, repeat the candle motif, making sure they are standing in the correct direction. Then reverse the stripe pattern, ending with 0.5 inches (1.25 cm) of plain weave and hem stitching. I left a 3-inch (7.5-cm) border of fringe at both ends. If you prefer, you can weave 1.5 inches (3.75 cm) of plain weave at each end and finish with a rolled hem.

This is a short warp to put on, so you might consider adding another yard and weaving two runners—one to keep and one to give away.

Now the flames! I embroidered the flames using satin stitches for the center and cross-stitch for the outer portion of the flame. Be careful not to pull your threads tight as you embroider because the woven threads move freely and will bunch up. I used three strands of floss, which filled the flames nicely.

Dimensions: 17 inches × 26 inches, plus 3-inch fringe (43.25 × 66 cm, 7.5-cm fringe)

Warp

Sett: 24 epi, 12 dent reed, 2 threads per dent
Length: 2-yard (1.8-m) warp
Threads: 10/2 perle cotton, White: 396 ends, 825 yards (754.4 m)
5/2 perle cotton, Royal Blue: 16 ends plus 2 floating selvedges = 18 ends, 45 yards (41.2 m)

Weft

Tabby: 10/2 perle cotton, White: 400 yards (365.8 m)
5/2 perle cotton
- Royal Blue: 60 yards (54.9 m)
- Gold by Lunatic Fringe: 15 yards (13.7 m)

DMC floss for embroidered flames:
- 972 (dark color): 1 skein
- 726 (light color): 1 skein

Border 1
12 ends

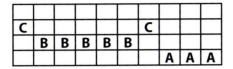

Motif A
40 ends

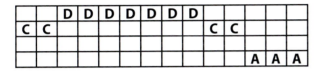

Motif B
56 ends

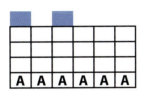

Border 2
24 ends

Threading
Border 1: 1 time
Motif A: 4 times
Motif B: 1 time
Motif A: 4 times
Border 2: 1 time

Treadling
Follow instructions in text on page 123. Add tabby after each pattern thread.

						T	T	
							6	
5	5	5	5				5	
4	4						4	
3	3	3	3	3	3		3	
	2		2		2	2		
1		1		1		1		
						X		Tabby
							X	
				X				
					X			
				X				Base of candle Gold
					X			
				X				
					X			
				X				
			X					Body of all candles Repeat 12X
		X						
	X							Body of tall candle Repeat 6X
X								

Blue

HANUKKAH RUNNER | 125

Bunches of Bunnies Blanket

What a fun gift for the expectant family! The use of multiple colors makes this piece the perfect blanket for either a boy or a girl. I can envision this blanket in many different combinations—have fun using colors to make it uniquely yours. For the bunnies, I chose to match the colors in the variegated thread. The maize bunny turned out very light, so feel free to change that to another color if you prefer. I used a single strand of 8/2 cotton for the bunnies, but if you double your thread, it will make the bunnies stand out more.

Begin the blanket with 4 inches (10.25 cm) of plain weave with the variegated thread. Next, you will start weaving the first bunny section. Weave eight passes of White plain weave and then begin to weave the first bunny. Be sure to study the treadling chart so your bunnies are standing correctly. Also follow each pattern thread with a tabby thread. After you have woven your bunny, weave eight more passes of plain weave.

Next, you create the segue, which is as follows: eight passes of variegated, four passes of White, eight passes of variegated. After that, weave the second bunny. After the second bunny, weave 25 inches (63.5 cm) of plain weave with the variegated fiber. Next, weave two more sets of bunnies, being sure to include the segue pattern. Finish the blanket with 4 inches (10.25 cm) of plain weave in variegated fiber. Complete the blanket with a rolled hem on each end. You could weave the entire blanket with bunnies for something different. Have fun!

Dimensions: 35 inches × 48 inches (88.9 × 121.9 cm)

Warp
Sett: 20 epi, 10 dent reed, 2 threads per dent
Length: 2.75-yard (2.5-m) warp
8/2 Cotton Clouds variegated, Rainbow: 24 ends plus 2 floating selvedges = 26 ends, 75 yards (68.5 m)
8/2 Cotton Clouds, White: 672 ends, 1,875 yards (1,714.5 m)

Weft
Tabby: 8/2 Cotton Clouds, White: 500 yards (457.2 m)
8/2 cotton (all colors by Cotton Clouds)
- Rainbow (variegated): 750 yards (685.8 m)
- Duck: 50 yards (45.7 m)
- Beauty Rose: 50 yards (45.7 m)
- Maize: 50 yards (45.7 m)
- Dark Turk: 50 yards (45.7 m)

Threading

Border: 3 times
Full Motif: 21 times
Border: 3 times

Treadling

Follow instructions in text on page 127. Add tabby after each pattern thread.

128 | BUNCHES OF BUNNIES BLANKET

Just a Wrap

This is a very versatile piece. The warp is longer than generally allowed for a scarf but not as long as for a shawl. Creating this piece out of Tencel gives it a wonderful drape, which is perfect for all of the ways you can use it. It's long enough to wrap around your head on a windy day and protect your ears, though not so wide that you can't wear it as a scarf and show off some fancy knotting techniques. And it is just wide enough to cover your shoulders if you get chilled. This wrap just might become one of your favorite pieces in your wardrobe.

Begin and end with 0.5 inches (1.25 cm) of plain weave and hem stitching. Since Tencel tends to fray, it is best to twist the fringe. For the floating selvedges, use two strands of the Tencel to prevent breakage.

Dimensions: 14 inches × 70 inches, plus 4-inch fringe
(35.6 × 177.8 cm, 10.25-cm fringe)

Warp
Sett: 20 epi, 10 dent reed, 2 threads per dent
Length: 3.25-yard (3-m) warp
Thread: 8/2 Tencel, Blue/Purple: 284 ends plus 4 floating selvedges = 288 ends, 950 yards (868.7 m)

Weft
8/2 Tencel, Silver Gray: 600 yards (548.6 m)
Tabby: 8/2 Tencel, Blue/Purple: 600 yards (548.6 m)

Partial Motif
4 ends

Full Motif
40 ends

Threading
Full Motif: 7 times
Partial Motif: 1 time

Partial Motif to Balance

Treadling
Repeat Full Motif to desired length.
End with Partial Motif.
Add tabby after each pattern thread.

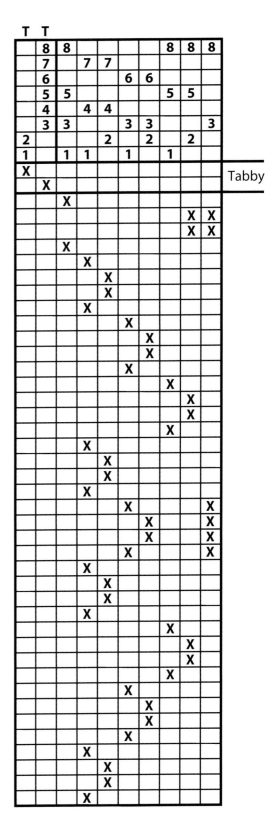

Full Motif

JUST A WRAP | 131

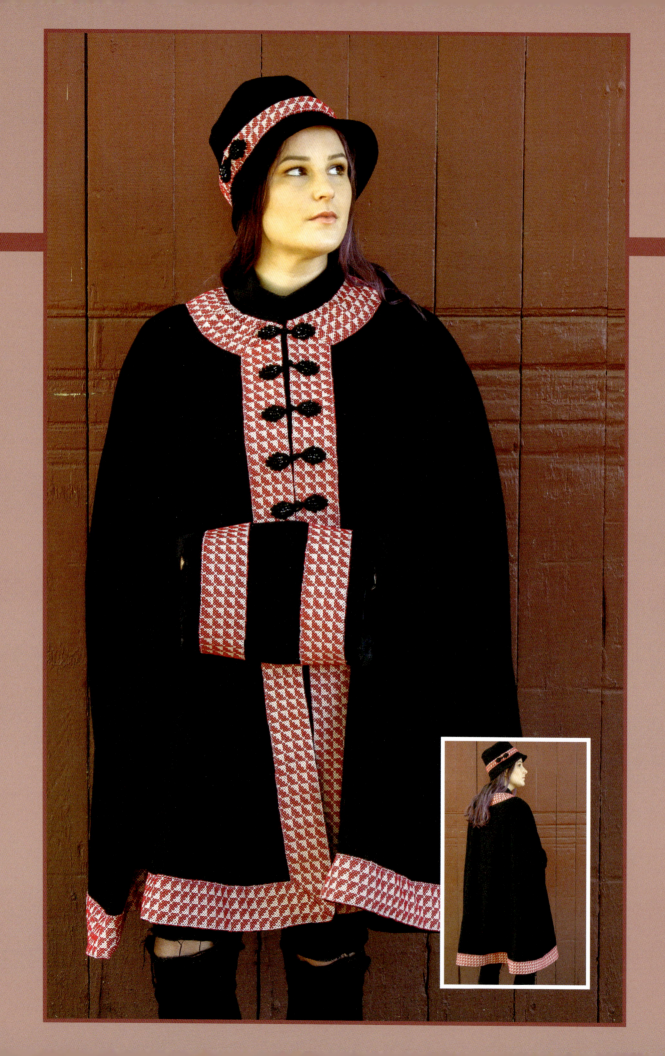

Going in Style Trim

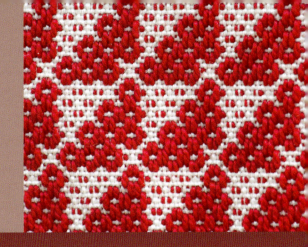

So many times as weavers we think we have to weave the entire project: a scarf or shawl, for example. But that's not always true. Think outside the box. Instead of weaving another shawl or scarf, weave trim to embellish a piece. This can be something you have sewn yourself or a purchased garment or bag.

For this set, I sewed a 100% wool black cape, matching cloche hat, and a faux fur–lined muff. I determined the yardage I would need to trim these pieces and added a bit more, just to be safe. For this set, I used a 10-yard (9.1-m) warp. Once the weaving was done, I trimmed the cape and hat and then trimmed and sewed the muff. I folded the trim for the hat so it would fit better. This set makes a wonderful collection and will definitely be noticed when worn. You could easily trim just the bottom of your favorite jacket or a warm set of mittens. There are so many options. Adding trim to purchased items is another way to create a special wedding or shower gift.

I have given you the basic threading, treadling, and tie-up for this pattern. I did four repeats of the threading to get the width I desired. The width will vary with your thread choices and how wide you want your piece to be. And then I just wove as far as I could on the warp. The yardage requirements were for *my* project, so your requirements may be different. Yes, this can get a bit tedious for a long warp, but break it down to manageable amounts. I weave a minimum of 20 inches (50.8 cm) a day, and before long, I am done.

Dimensions: 2.5 inches (6.25 cm) wide; approx. 9 yards (8.2 m) trim

Warp
Sett: 24 epi, 12 dent reed, 2 threads per dent
Length: 10-yard (9.1-m) warp
Thread: 10/2 perle cotton, Natural: 64 ends plus 2 floating selvedges = 66 ends, 700 yards (640.1 m)

Weft
5/2 perle cotton, Lipstick: 600 yards (548.6 m)
Tabby: 10/2 perle cotton, Natural: 600 yards (548.6 m)

Threading and Treadling

Repeat threading and treadling to desired width and length.

D			
	C		
		B	
			A

Full Motif
16 ends

T	T								
	6	6	6	6	6	6	6		
	5	5	5	5	5				
	4	4	4						
	3							3	3
2			2		2		2		2
1		1		1		1		1	
X									
	X									Tabby
		X							
			X						
			X						
		X							
				X					
					X				
					X				
				X					
						X			
							X		
							X		
						X			
								X	
									X
									X
								X	

Full Motif

134 | GOING IN STYLE TRIM

RESOURCES

8-Shaft Patterns by Carol Strickler. Interweave Press: Loveland, Colorado.
A Handweaver's Pattern Book by Marguerite P. Davison. Spencer Graphics, Inc.
The Handweaver's Pattern Directory by Anne Dixon. Interweave Press: Loveland, Colorado.

Cotton Clouds, Inc: Payson, Arizona. https://cottonclouds.com/
Red Stone Glen Fiber Arts Center: Tom Knisely, York Haven, Pennsylvania. https://redstoneglen.com/
Robyn Spady: https://www.spadystudios.com/

OTHER WEAVING BOOKS BY SUSAN KESLER-SIMPSON

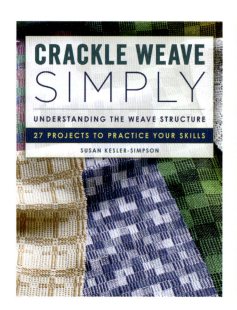
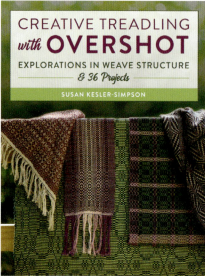
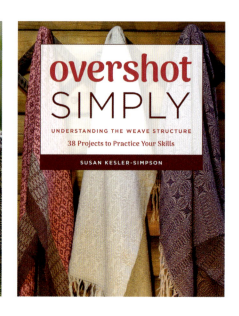
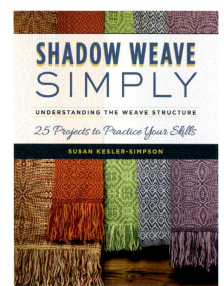
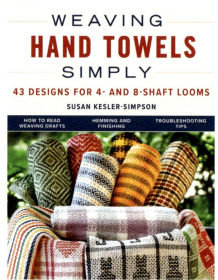